Vegan Italiano

50 FRESH PLANT-BASED RECIPES FROM <u>LAKE COMO</u>

AUTHENTIC ITALIAN FLAVORS REIMAGINED

BY MANUELE COLOMBO

TABLE OF
CONTENTS

Ciao!

Welcome to Vegan Italiano: 50 Fresh Plant-Based Recipes from Lake Como!

I am Manuele Colombo, a passionate home cook from the stunning shores of Lake Como. My love for Italian cuisine and a plant-based lifestyle has inspired me to reimagine the rich traditions of Italian cooking with fresh, vibrant, and wholesome ingredients. Through these recipes, I aim to show that the heart and soul of Italian food—its depth, flavor, and heritage—can thrive beautifully in a plant-based kitchen.

In this cookbook, I invite you to join me on a journey to discover how the timeless charm of Italian cuisine can embrace a plant-based approach. Whether you're a seasoned cook, new to vegan food, or simply looking to enjoy more plant-based meals, this book offers recipes that are easy to follow, delicious, and true to the authentic flavors of Italy.

Inside Vegan Italiano, you'll find dishes that capture the essence of Italian dining:

- Begin with **Antipasti**, like crispy Polenta Bites with Sun-Dried Tomato Pesto or Fried Zucchini Blossoms stuffed with Almond Ricotta.
- Indulge in **Primi Piatti**, such as creamy Vegan Pumpkin Gnocchi with Brown Butter Sage Sauce or hearty Spinach and Mushroom Lasagna with Cashew Ricotta.
- Savor **Secondi Piatti**, like Tofu Piccata in a Lemon-Caper Sauce or a robust Lentil Bolognese with Rigatoni.
- Complement your meals with **Contorni**, vibrant sides such as Rosemary and Olive Oil Roasted Potatoes or Sautéed Spinach with Pine Nuts and Raisins.
- And don't miss **Dolci**, sweet treats like a decadent Vegan Tiramisu or a zesty Lemon Almond Ricotta Cake to round off your meal.

This book is my tribute to the evolving landscape of Italian cuisine, where tradition meets innovation in a way that is both exciting and nourishing. I hope these recipes inspire you to gather around the table with loved ones, try new flavors, and create memorable meals full of joy and warmth.

If you love these recipes, visit my website, _FreshPlantBased.com_, for more ideas, tips, and inspiration for plant-based cooking!

Buon appetito and welcome to Vegan Italiano!

The Timeless Charm of Lake Como

Nestled in the foothills of the **Italian Alps, Lake Como** is a place of unparalleled beauty, where **nature and history** intertwine to create a destination unlike any other. Renowned worldwide for its **pristine waters, dramatic mountain backdrops,** and **picturesque villages,** Lake Como has captivated travelers for centuries. Artists, poets, and royalty have found inspiration here, and today it continues to enchant visitors with its **timeless charm.** From the vibrant **gardens of Bellagio** to the serene **promenades of Varenna,** every corner of the lake seems touched by magic, offering **tranquility and elegance** in equal measure.

Adding to its allure, **Lake Como has become a favorite location for Hollywood filmmakers,** drawn by its **cinematic landscapes** and historic villas. **Blockbuster hits** such as Star Wars: Episode II - Attack of the Clones and Casino Royale were filmed here, showcasing the majestic **Villa Balbianello,** one of the lake's most iconic landmarks. The villa's terrace, with its sweeping views of the shimmering lake, became the backdrop for **Anakin and Padmé's romantic moments** in Star Wars, while its elegant halls hosted scenes with **James Bond** himself in *Casino Royale.* Other notable films, including *Ocean's Twelve* and *Murder Mystery,* have also captured the lake's grandeur, solidifying its place in the imagination of **movie lovers worldwide.**

Among the lake's treasures, **Villa Balbianello** stands as a crown jewel. Perched on a verdant **peninsula** that gently extends into the lake, this historic villa is a harmonious blend of **architecture and natural beauty.** Its **manicured gardens,** adorned with statues and blooming pergolas, invite visitors to step into another era, where time seems to stand still. The **panoramic views** from the villa are breathtaking, offering a serene escape from the modern world and a reminder of the **enduring beauty** of this special place.

It's easy to understand why **Lake Como** and its surroundings inspire not only **filmmakers** and travelers but also **chefs and food lovers.** This cookbook captures the essence of the lake's enchanting atmosphere through vibrant, **plant-based recipes** that celebrate **Italy's culinary traditions.** Each dish in this book is a tribute to the **fresh, seasonal ingredients** that are at the heart of Italian cooking—an invitation to bring the **spirit of Lake Como** to your kitchen.

As you savor these recipes, let them transport you to the lake's tranquil shores. Imagine dining **al fresco** on a warm evening, surrounded by the gentle rustle of olive trees and the shimmering reflection of the water. Let the **timeless beauty of Lake Como** inspire your cooking and remind you of the joy that comes from gathering around the table with loved ones.

Buon appetito!

Photo on the side: Villa Balbianello, Lake Como

Introduction

This cookbook, Vegan Italiano: 50 Fresh Plant-Based Recipes from Lake Como, is designed to immerse you in the authentic Italian dining experience through a plant-based lens. Structured in the traditional Italian meal progression, each chapter mirrors the way a typical Italian meal unfolds, guiding you from vibrant appetizers to hearty main courses, and ending with sweet, indulgent desserts.

If you enjoy these recipes, I warmly invite you to visit my website, _FreshPlantBased.com_, for even more plant-based ideas, tips, and inspiration to enhance your cooking journey!

Chapter 1: Antipasti (Appetizers)
The Italian meal traditionally begins with antipasti, light bites that awaken the palate. This chapter offers vegan takes on classics like Crispy Polenta Bites with Sun-Dried Tomato Pesto, Roasted Bell Pepper Bruschetta, and Vegan Caprese Skewers. These colorful, flavorful dishes set the perfect tone for any gathering.

Chapter 2: Primi Piatti (First Courses)
Primi piatti introduce comforting dishes like pasta, risotto, and soups. In this chapter, enjoy creamy, plant-based versions of favorites such as Zucchini Noodle Carbonara with smoky tempeh, Vegan Butternut Squash Risotto, and hearty Tuscan White Bean Soup with Kale. Each recipe blends rich flavors with a vegan twist, staying true to Italian tradition.

Chapter 3: Secondi Piatti (Main Courses)
Secondi piatti, the main course, often feature bold and satisfying dishes. Here, you'll discover plant-based delights like Eggplant Involtini Stuffed with Cashew Ricotta, Vegan Osso Buco with Jackfruit, and Portobello Mushroom Marsala. These recipes deliver depth and richness, offering delicious alternatives to classic Italian mains.

Chapter 4: Contorni (Side Dishes)
Contorni, or side dishes, complement the main course with simple yet flavorful vegetable dishes and salads. This chapter includes recipes like Grilled Asparagus with Lemon Zest, Rosemary and Olive Oil Roasted Potatoes, and a fresh Vegan Caesar Salad with Crispy Chickpeas. These sides bring balance and variety to your table.

Chapter 5: Dolci (Desserts)
Italian meals conclude with dolci, sweet indulgences that leave a lasting impression. In this chapter, you'll find vegan desserts that embody Italian elegance, such as Vegan Tiramisu with Coconut Cream, Almond Biscotti Dipped in Dark Chocolate, and a zesty Lemon Almond Ricotta Cake. These recipes provide the perfect finale to any meal.

With Vegan Italiano, my goal is to bring Italy's cherished culinary traditions into your home, reimagined for a plant-based lifestyle. I hope this book inspires you to create meals that are as authentic as they are innovative, celebrating the best of Italian cuisine.

If you love what you find here, be sure to visit _FreshPlantBased.com_ for more recipes, tips, and ideas to continue your plant-based culinary journey.

Buon appetito!

Exploring the Treasures of the Tremezzina

The Tremezzina area, a captivating stretch along the western shores of **Lake Como,** is a haven of natural beauty, historic charm, and tranquil elegance. This region encompasses picturesque villages like **Tremezzo, Lenno, and Mezzegra,** each offering its own slice of paradise. Tremezzo is home to the world-famous **Villa Carlotta**, celebrated for its stunning **botanical gardens** filled with vibrant azaleas, camellias, and rare plants. This majestic villa, with its rich history and breathtaking views of the lake, hosted one of the **2018 Dolce & Gabbana fashion shows,** further solidifying its reputation as a symbol of Italian elegance.

Not far from Villa Carlotta, the **Parco Civico Teresio Olivelli** offers a serene lakeside retreat, complete with its graceful fountain and meandering pathways. This picturesque park also served as a glamorous backdrop for another **Dolce & Gabbana show**, blending haute couture with the timeless beauty of the lake.

In **Lenno,** the enchanting **Golfo di Venere** (Gulf of Venus) frames the tranquil harbor, providing access to the iconic **Villa Balbianello,** perched on a lush promontory. Just a short boat ride away, you'll find **Isola Comacina,** the only island on Lake Como, steeped in history and mystery. Whether exploring grand villas, enjoying a lakeside aperitivo, or simply soaking in the vistas, the Tremezzina region invites you to immerse yourself in its timeless allure.

Photo on the side: Tremezzo Village, Lake Como

Bellagio: The Pearl of Lake Como

Known as the **"Pearl of Lake Como," Bellagio** is one of the most renowned and picturesque destinations in Italy. Perfectly situated at the meeting point of the lake's three branches, Bellagio offers breathtaking panoramic views of the shimmering waters and the majestic Alps in the distance. Its cobblestone streets, elegant villas, and vibrant waterfront promenade have made it a symbol of timeless beauty and sophistication.

Bellagio's global fame extends far beyond Italy, inspiring the design of the opulent **Bellagio Hotel and Casino in Las Vegas,** which pays homage to its enchanting Italian namesake. While the hotel's fountains and grandeur capture some of Bellagio's essence, nothing compares to the charm of the original. From strolling through the **Villa Melzi Gardens,** with their manicured landscapes and historic sculptures, to enjoying a gelato in the lively town square, Bellagio is the epitome of elegance and Italian hospitality.

For visitors, Bellagio represents the perfect blend of history, luxury, and natural beauty—an iconic destination that embodies the magic of Lake Como. Its timeless allure makes it not just a place to visit, but an experience to treasure.

Photo on the side: Streets of Bellagio with lake view, Lake Como

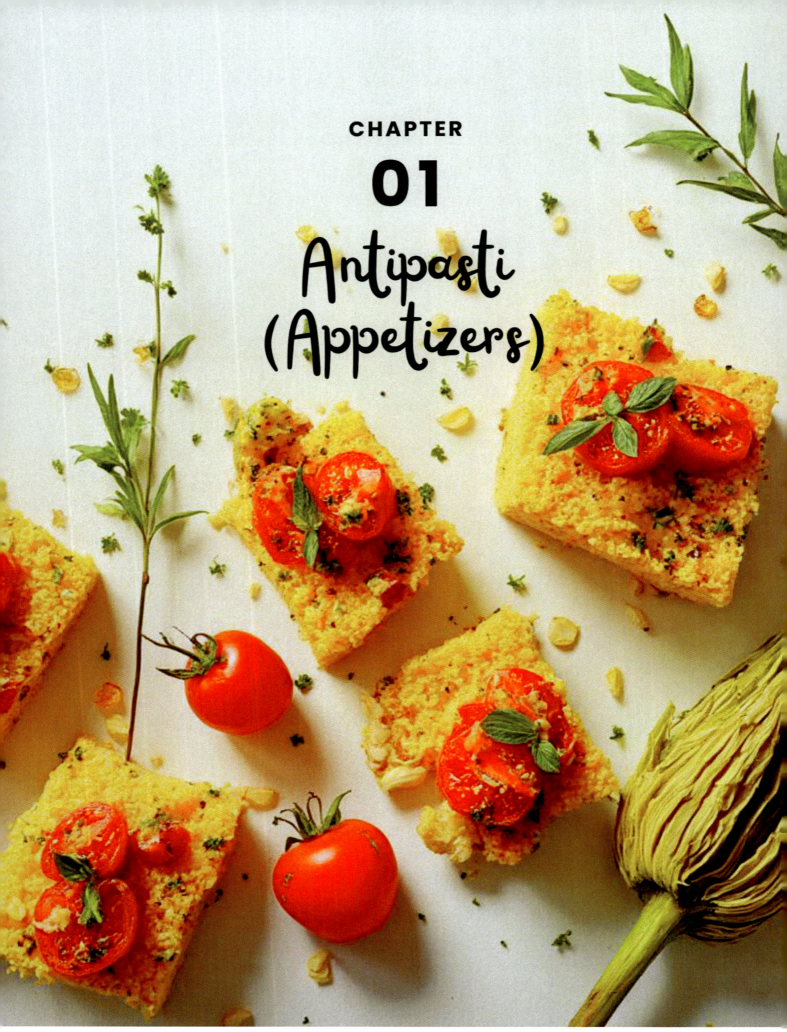

CHAPTER

01

Antipasti
(Appetizers)

Overview

Antipasti (literally, "before the meal") introduces diners to an Italian meal with an array of small bites that excite the senses and prepare the palate. This chapter offers vegan renditions of classic Italian starters, all rich in flavor and texture. These recipes celebrate fresh vegetables, herbs, and the art of simple but impactful dishes that entice everyone at the table.

Discover more Antipasti recipes and inspiration at ***FreshPlantBased.com***!

Crispy Polenta Bites with Sun-Dried Tomato Pesto

Imagine biting into a golden, crispy polenta square with a soft, creamy center, topped with a rich, tangy sun-dried tomato pesto. This appetizer brings the warmth and richness of Italian flavors to life in a small, delicious bite. Perfect for a dinner party or a casual gathering, these polenta bites celebrate the simplicity of Italian ingredients, offering an elegant yet satisfying snack. Paired with a fresh Italian white wine, each bite is an invitation to savor the essence of Italy.

Wine Pairing: Pinot Grigio or a Sauvignon Blanc

Difficulty

20 min   30 min

INGREDIENTS

4 servings

For the Polenta:
1 cup polenta (coarse cornmeal)
4 cups water
1 tsp sea salt
2 tbsp olive oil

For the Sun-Dried Tomato Pesto:
1 cup sun-dried tomatoes (oil-packed, drained)
1/2 cup fresh basil leaves
1/4 cup pine nuts (or walnuts)
2 cloves garlic, minced
1/4 cup olive oil
Salt and pepper to taste

Allergens

CONTAINS NUTS

INSTRUCTIONS

Prepare the Polenta:
- Boil 4 cups of water with 1 teaspoon sea salt.
- Whisk in polenta slowly; reduce heat to low, stirring to avoid lumps.
- Cook for 25-30 minutes until thick and creamy, pulling away from the pan sides.
- Stir in 2 tablespoons olive oil for a glossy finish.
- Pour into an 8x8-inch dish, smoothing the top, and let cool for about an hour.

Cut and Fry the Polenta Bites:
- Cut set polenta into 1.5-inch squares.
- Heat olive oil in a skillet over medium heat; fry squares in batches for 3-4 minutes per side until golden and crispy.
- Drain on paper towels.

Prepare the Sun-Dried Tomato Pesto:
- In a food processor, blend sun-dried tomatoes, basil, pine nuts, and garlic until finely chopped.
- With the processor running, drizzle in olive oil until spreadable; season with salt and pepper.

Assemble the Bites:
- Top each crispy polenta square with sun-dried tomato pesto, garnish with basil or lemon zest.
- Serve warm or at room temperature.

CHEF'S TIPS

Extra Flavor Add a sprinkle of nutritional yeast to the polenta mixture for a nutty, cheesy flavor that pairs beautifully with the tomato pesto.

Variations: For a touch of spice, mix a pinch of red pepper flakes into the pesto.

Roasted Bell Pepper Bruschetta

Few appetizers capture the essence of Italian flavors quite like bruschetta. This Roasted Bell Pepper Bruschetta combines the sweetness of roasted bell peppers with the earthy taste of garlic and the fresh aroma of basil. With each bite, you'll experience the vibrant flavors of Italy, brought together on a crisp piece of toasted bread. Perfect for any occasion, this simple yet flavorful bruschetta will impress your guests and leave them wanting more.

Wine Pairing: Vermentino or a Pinot Grigio

Difficulty

15 min   30 min

INGREDIENTS

4 servings

4 large bell peppers (red, yellow, or a mix)
1/4 cup extra virgin olive oil, plus extra for drizzling
2 cloves garlic, minced
1 tbsp balsamic vinegar
Salt and pepper to taste
1/4 cup fresh basil leaves, chopped
1 baguette, sliced into 1/2-inch slices
Fresh basil leaves for garnish (optional)

Allergens

CONTAINS GLUTEN

INSTRUCTIONS

Roasting Bell Peppers:

- Preheat oven to 450°F (230°C).
- Roast bell peppers on a baking sheet for 25-30 minutes, turning every 10 minutes until charred and soft.
- Transfer to a bowl, cover with plastic wrap, and steam for 10 minutes to ease skin removal.
- Once cooled, peel, remove seeds, and slice into thin strips.

Preparing Marinated Bell Peppers:

- Combine roasted pepper strips with 1/4 cup olive oil, minced garlic, balsamic vinegar, salt, and pepper in a bowl.
- Toss and stir in chopped fresh basil; marinate for at least 15 minutes.

Toasting Bread:

- Preheat oven to 400°F (200°C).
- Arrange baguette slices on a baking sheet, drizzle with olive oil, and toast for 5-7 minutes until golden.

Assembling Bruschetta:

- Spoon marinated bell pepper mixture onto toasted baguette slices.

Optionally garnish with fresh basil.
Serve immediately for a delightful flavor balance.

CHEF'S TIPS

Extra Flavor: For a hint of smoky flavor, consider grilling the bread slices instead of toasting them in the oven.

Variations: Add vegan feta for creaminess or more balsamic vinegar for depth.

Stuffed Cherry Tomatoes with Herbed Cashew Cheese

These Stuffed Cherry Tomatoes with Herbed Cashew Cheese are a delightful bite-sized appetizer that bursts with fresh, creamy, and savory flavors. The sweetness of juicy cherry tomatoes pairs perfectly with the smooth, herb-infused cashew cheese, creating a refreshing and satisfying taste. Perfect for entertaining or as an elegant starter to a larger meal, these stuffed tomatoes are sure to impress with both their look and taste.

Wine Pairing: Prosecco or a Sparkling Wine

Difficulty

20 min

INGREDIENTS

4 servings

For the Herbed Cashew Cheese:
1 cup raw cashews (soaked in water for at least 2 hours)
1 tbsp lemon juice
1 clove garlic, minced
2 tbsp nutritional yeast
1/4 cup water (add more if needed for consistency)
Salt to taste
2 tbsp fresh chives, chopped
1 tbsp fresh parsley, chopped

For the Tomatoes:
1 pint cherry tomatoes
Fresh basil leaves for garnish (optional)

Allergens

CONTAINS NUTS

INSTRUCTIONS

Prepare Cashew Cheese:
- Drain and rinse soaked cashews.
- Blend with lemon juice, minced garlic, nutritional yeast, and 1/4 cup water until smooth, adding more water as needed.
- Season with salt and fold in chopped chives and parsley.
- Refrigerate for 10 minutes to meld flavors.

Prepare Cherry Tomatoes:
- Slice tops off cherry tomatoes and scoop out seeds and pulp to create hollow centers.
- Set aside on a platter.

Fill Tomatoes:
- Use a piping bag or resealable bag to fill each tomato with cashew cheese.

Garnish and Serve:
- Top with a basil leaf or extra chives.
- Serve chilled for best flavor.

CHEF'S TIPS

Extra Flavor: For a touch of zest, add a pinch of lemon zest to the cashew cheese mixture. It enhances the brightness of the filling and complements the tomatoes beautifully.

Variations: Incorporate chopped olives or sun-dried tomatoes for a Mediterranean flavor.

Marinated Olives with Lemon and Rosemary

Imagine a vibrant platter of glistening olives infused with the sunny zest of lemon and the earthy warmth of rosemary. This simple yet richly flavored appetizer brings together the best of Mediterranean aromas in a single bite. Marinated olives are an iconic Italian treat, perfect for adding a touch of elegance to any table setting. Each olive carries a burst of fresh, herbal notes, balanced by the slight tang of lemon, making this dish both refreshing and deeply satisfying. It's an effortless way to capture the essence of Italy in a small, delightful appetizer.

Wine Pairing: Chianti or a Zinfandel

Difficulty

10 min

INGREDIENTS

4 servings

2 cups mixed olives (green, black, or a blend of your favorites)
Zest of 1 lemon, peeled into strips
Juice of 1/2 lemon
2 cloves garlic, thinly sliced
2 sprigs fresh rosemary
1/4 cup extra virgin olive oil
1/2 tsp red pepper flakes
(optional, for a hint of heat)
Freshly ground black pepper, to taste

Allergens

INSTRUCTIONS

Prepare the Marinade:
In a medium bowl, mix lemon zest, lemon juice, garlic, rosemary, and olive oil. Add red pepper flakes for spice and stir to combine.

Add the Olives:
Incorporate mixed olives into the marinade, gently coating them. Season with freshly ground black pepper to taste.

Marinate:
Cover and let olives marinate at room temperature for at least 1 hour or up to 24 hours in the refrigerator for deeper flavor. Bring to room temperature before serving.

Serve and Enjoy:
Transfer marinated olives to a serving bowl, garnishing with lemon zest and rosemary. Serve with crusty bread or as part of an antipasto platter.

CHEF'S TIPS

Extra Flavor: Lightly warm olive oil with garlic and rosemary to enhance their aroma before adding to the marinade.

Variations: Include fresh orange zest for sweetness or fennel seeds for a subtle aniseed flavor.

Vegan Caprese Skewers

Picture a skewer adorned with the vivid hues of an Italian summer: ruby-red grape tomatoes, fragrant green basil, and creamy tofu cubes that mimic fresh mozzarella. These Vegan Caprese Skewers encapsulate the spirit of a traditional Caprese salad in a delightful, bite-sized treat. The tofu is marinated to achieve a subtle, cheesy tang, while the basil infuses a refreshing burst of flavor in every bite. Ideal for gatherings or as a light appetizer, these skewers are not only delicious but also visually captivating, delivering authentic Italian flavors right to your table.

Wine Pairing: Pinot Grigio or a Sauvignon Blanc

Difficulty

15 min

INGREDIENTS

4 servings

1 cup firm tofu, cut into 1-inch cubes
1 tbsp extra virgin olive oil
1 tbsp apple cider vinegar or lemon juice
1/2 tsp sea salt
1/4 tsp freshly ground black pepper
1 cup grape tomatoes
Fresh basil leaves
Balsamic glaze, for drizzling (optional)

Allergens

CONTAINS SOY

INSTRUCTIONS

Marinate the Tofu
- In a small bowl, whisk together the olive oil, apple cider vinegar (or lemon juice), sea salt, and black pepper.
- Add the tofu cubes to the bowl, tossing gently to ensure each piece is well-coated. Allow the tofu to marinate for at least 30 minutes to absorb the flavors. This step imparts a subtle tang that mimics fresh mozzarella.

Prepare the Skewers
- Once the tofu is marinated, start assembling the skewers. Begin by threading a grape tomato onto a small skewer or toothpick, followed by a fresh basil leaf, a cube of marinated tofu, and another grape tomato.
- Repeat the process for each skewer until all ingredients are used.

Serve
- Arrange the completed skewers on a serving platter. For an extra touch of flavor and visual appeal, drizzle lightly with balsamic glaze if desired. The balsamic's sweetness complements the tomato and basil, elevating the dish to a delightful harmony of flavors.

CHEF'S TIPS

Extra Flavor: Add nutritional yeast to the marinade for a stronger cheesy flavor.

Variations: Use colorful heirloom cherry tomatoes for visual appeal and sprinkle with sea salt before serving to enhance flavor.

Carciofi alla Romana (Roman-Style Artichokes)

Carciofi alla Romana features tender artichokes filled with fresh mint, parsley, and garlic, simmered in rich olive oil. This classic Roman dish combines the rustic beauty of artichokes with aromatic herbs, resulting in a flavorful and textured experience. Each bite offers a taste of Rome, making it a delightful appetizer or side that highlights simplicity and elegance.

Wine Pairing: Vermentino or a Sauvignon Blanc

Difficulty

20 min   25 min

INGREDIENTS

4 servings

4 large artichokes (preferably Roman purple artichokes, but other varieties work well)
1 cup fresh mint leaves (mentuccia romana if available)
1 cup fresh parsley leaves
2 cloves garlic, minced
1/2 cup extra virgin olive oil (use a high-quality, fragrant oil)
1 lemon
1 cup water
1 tbsp salt (adjust at the end if needed)
1 tbsp freshly ground black pepper

Allergens

INSTRUCTIONS

Prepare the Lemon Water:
- Cut lemon in half and fill a large bowl with water.
- Squeeze half the lemon into the bowl to create a lemon-water bath to prevent artichokes from browning.

Trim the Artichokes:
- Trim the stem and top tip of each artichoke.
- Spread petals to expose the core, peel the stem, and scoop out the inedible choke.

Soak the Artichokes:
- Submerge cleaned artichokes in the lemon-water bath and cover with a cloth to keep them submerged.

Make the Herb Filling:
- Chop mint and parsley, then combine with minced garlic, salt, and pepper in a bowl.

Stuff the Artichokes:
- Remove artichokes from lemon water, shake off excess, and fill the cores with the herb mixture.

Cook the Artichokes:
- Place stuffed artichokes upside down in a pan, pour olive oil and water over them.

Simmer and Serve:
- Cover and cook on low heat for 20-25 minutes until tender. Serve warm or at room temperature with crusty Italian bread.

CHEF'S TIPS

Extra Flavor: Add nutritional yeast to the marinade for a stronger cheesy flavor.

Variations: Use colorful heirloom cherry tomatoes for visual appeal and sprinkle with sea salt before serving to enhance flavor.

Fried Zucchini Blossoms Stuffed with Almond Ricotta

Fried Zucchini Blossoms are a delicacy that captures the essence of Italian summer in each crispy, golden bite. These delicate, edible flowers are carefully stuffed with a creamy almond ricotta that's rich, savory, and entirely plant-based. Once fried to perfection, the blossoms have a crisp exterior that gives way to a soft, decadent filling. Each bite is a delightful balance of texture and flavor—a wonderful combination of fresh zucchini blossom and luscious almond ricotta. Served warm, they're a stunning and delicious appetizer that's sure to impress.

Wine Pairing: Prosecco or a Sparkling Wine

Difficulty

20 min   10 min

INGREDIENTS

4 servings

For the Almond Ricotta:
1 cup blanched almonds (soaked in water for at least 2 hours, then drained)
1 tbsp lemon juice
1 clove garlic, minced
1/4 cup water (or more as needed for consistency)
Salt, to taste

For the Zucchini Blossoms:
12 zucchini blossoms
1/2 cup all-purpose flour
3/4 cup sparkling water, chilled
Salt, to taste
Oil for frying (such as vegetable or sunflower oil)

Allergens

CONTAINS GLUTEN   CONTAINS NUTS

INSTRUCTIONS

Prepare Almond Ricotta:
- Blend soaked almonds, lemon juice, garlic, and salt until combined.
- Gradually add water for a creamy texture.
- Adjust seasoning and transfer to a bowl.

Stuff Zucchini Blossoms:
- Open each blossom and fill with almond ricotta using a spoon or piping bag.
- Twist tips to secure filling.

Prepare Batter:
- Whisk flour, salt, and chilled sparkling water until smooth.

Fry Blossoms:
- Heat 1 inch of oil over medium-high heat.
- Test oil with a bit of batter; it should sizzle.
- Dip stuffed blossoms in batter and fry for 2-3 minutes per side until golden and crispy.
- Use a slotted spoon to transfer to paper towels.

Serve:
- Arrange fried blossoms on a platter and garnish with sea salt or fresh basil. Serve immediately for best flavor and crispness.

CHEF'S TIPS

Extra Flavor: Add nutritional yeast to almond ricotta for cheesy umami.

Variations: Mix in chopped fresh chili or red pepper flakes for spice.

Eggplant Caponata Crostini

Eggplant Caponata Crostini captures the essence of Sicily in a vibrant, sweet, and tangy relish served atop crispy crostini. This dish is an explosion of colors and textures, with the rich purple of roasted eggplant, the deep green of olives, and the pop of red from ripe tomatoes. Each bite is a symphony of flavors—sweet, savory, and slightly acidic—that lingers on the palate. This vegan appetizer is perfect for a casual get-together or an elegant starter, bringing the warmth of Mediterranean flavors to your table.

Wine Pairing: Nero d'Avola or a Zinfandel

Difficulty

30 min   15 min

INGREDIENTS

4 servings

For the Caponata:
1 medium eggplant, diced into small cubes
1/4 cup olive oil, divided
1 small onion, finely chopped
2 cloves garlic, minced
1/4 cup green olives, chopped
2 tbsp capers, drained and rinsed
1/2 cup diced tomatoes
1 tbsp red wine vinegar
1 tbsp sugar (or maple syrup for a deeper flavor)
Salt and pepper, to taste
Fresh basil leaves, for garnish

For the Crostini:
1 baguette, sliced into 1/2-inch slices
Olive oil, for brushing

Allergens

CONTAINS GLUTEN

INSTRUCTIONS

Prepare the Crostini:
• Preheat oven to 400°F (200°C).
• Arrange baguette slices on a baking sheet, brush with olive oil.
• Toast for 8-10 minutes, until golden and crisp. Set aside.

Cook the Eggplant:
• Heat half the olive oil in a skillet over medium heat.
• Add diced eggplant, cook for 8-10 minutes until golden and tender. Set aside.

Make the Caponata:
• In the same skillet, add remaining olive oil, onion, and garlic. Cook until soft, about 5 minutes.
• Add olives, capers, tomatoes, and cooked eggplant. Stir in vinegar and sugar.
• Season, then simmer for 10-15 minutes until thick and glossy.

Assemble the Crostini:
• Spoon warm caponata onto each crostini. Garnish with fresh basil.

Serve:
• Arrange on a platter and serve warm or at room temperature.

CHEF'S TIPS

Extra Flavor: For a smoky twist, grill the eggplant before adding it to the caponata.

Variations: Add a handful of toasted pine nuts to the caponata just before serving for added texture and a touch of nuttiness.

Chickpea Fritters with Lemon Aioli

Golden and crispy on the outside, soft and flavorful on the inside, these Chickpea Fritters with Lemon Aioli are a perfect fusion of texture and taste. Inspired by the classic Italian panelle, these fritters are easy to make and full of savory goodness. The bright and zesty lemon aioli adds a refreshing contrast, enhancing every bite. Served warm, these fritters are ideal as an appetizer or a snack, inviting you to enjoy the simplicity and warmth of Italian street food in a modern, vegan twist.

Wine Pairing: Vermentino or a Pinot Grigio

Difficulty

20 min   15 min

INGREDIENTS

4 servings

For the Chickpea Fritters:
1 cup chickpea flour
1 1/2 cups water
Salt and pepper, to taste
1 tbsp fresh parsley, chopped
1 tbsp olive oil, plus extra for frying

For the Lemon Aioli:
1/2 cup vegan mayonnaise
Zest of 1 lemon
Juice of 1/2 lemon
1 clove garlic, finely minced
Salt and pepper, to taste

Allergens

INSTRUCTIONS

Prepare the Chickpea Fritter Batter:
- In a saucepan, whisk chickpea flour with water, salt, and pepper until smooth.
- Cook over medium heat, stirring often, until it thickens into a doughy mix (about 5-7 minutes).
- Add a splash of olive oil and chopped parsley, then spread on parchment to about 1/2-inch thickness. Let it cool until easy to handle.

Cut and Fry the Fritters:
- Cut the cooled batter into fun shapes—squares or triangles work great!
- Heat olive oil in a skillet and fry each piece for 2-3 minutes per side until crispy and golden.
- Let them rest on paper towels to absorb any extra oil.

Prepare the Lemon Aioli
- In a small bowl, stir together vegan mayo, lemon zest, lemon juice, garlic, salt, and pepper. Adjust with more lemon juice if you like extra zing.

Serve:
- Arrange the fritters on a platter with a bowl of lemon aioli for dipping. Garnish with parsley or a sprinkle of lemon zest for a fresh finish.

CHEF'S TIPS

Extra Flavor: Add a pinch of smoked paprika or cumin to the chickpea mixture for a smoky depth that complements the fritters beautifully.

Variations: For a Mediterranean twist, mix finely chopped sun-dried tomatoes or olives into the chickpea batter.

Vegan Pizzette (Mini Pizzas) with Olive Tapenade

Imagine a warm tray of mini pizzas, each topped with a spread of rich, briny olive tapenade and garnished with fresh basil. These Vegan Pizzette are perfect for any occasion, bringing together the flavors of a traditional Italian pizza in a fun, bite-sized form. The crisp, chewy crust and the bold olive tapenade offer a beautiful contrast, creating a satisfying bite that transports you to the sun-soaked Mediterranean coast. Ideal for gatherings or as an elegant appetizer, these pizzette are guaranteed to delight.

Wine Pairing: Chianti or a Merlot

Difficulty

25 min   12 min

INGREDIENTS

4 servings

For the Pizza Dough:
1 cup all-purpose flour (plus more for rolling)
1/2 tsp salt
1/2 cup warm water
1/2 tsp sugar
1/2 tsp active dry yeast
1 tbsp olive oil

For the Olive Tapenade:
1/2 cup black olives, pitted
1 tbsp capers
1 clove garlic, minced
1 tbsp olive oil
1 tsp lemon juice
Fresh basil leaves, for garnish

Allergens

CONTAINS GLUTEN

INSTRUCTIONS

Prepare the Dough:
• Mix warm water, sugar, and yeast; let sit until foamy.
• In a bowl, combine flour and salt, then add yeast mixture and olive oil. Stir, knead on a floured surface for 5-7 minutes until smooth.
• Let rise in an oiled bowl, covered, for 1 hour until doubled. Punch down and roll out, then cut into 2-inch circles.

Preheat Oven and Make Tapenade:
• Preheat oven to 400ºF (200ºC), line a baking sheet.
• Blend olives, capers, garlic, olive oil, and lemon juice in a food processor to a chunky paste.

Assemble and Bake:
• Place dough circles on the sheet, spread tapenade on each, leaving a border.
• Bake for 12-15 minutes until golden and crisp.

Garnish and Serve:
• Cool slightly, garnish with basil. Serve warm or at room temperature.

CHEF'S TIPS

Extra Flavor: Add a sprinkle of nutritional yeast to the tapenade mixture for a subtle cheesy flavor that complements the olives and capers.

Variations: Experiment with different toppings, like a dollop of sun-dried tomato spread or roasted red pepper strips, for added color and flavor.

CHAPTER
02
Primi Piatti
(First Courses)

Overview

Primi Piatti (first courses) are the heart of an Italian meal, showcasing comforting dishes like pasta, risotto, and soups. These recipes embody the richness and tradition of Italian cuisine while being entirely plant-based. From creamy sauces to hearty grains, this chapter highlights the balance of flavor and texture that makes Italian first courses so beloved.

Find more Primi Piatti ideas on *FreshPlantBased.com*!

Zucchini Noodle Carbonara

Zucchini Noodle Carbonara offers a plant-based twist on classic Italian carbonara. It features fresh zucchini noodles coated in a creamy, smoky cashew-based sauce with nutritional yeast and smoked paprika. Topped with crispy tempeh "bacon," this gluten-free and vegan dish balances creaminess, smokiness, and freshness while maintaining the comforting taste of traditional carbonara.

Wine Pairing: Pinot Grigio or a Chardonnay

Difficulty

20 min   25 min

INGREDIENTS

4 servings

For the Carbonara Sauce:
1 cup raw cashews, soaked in water for at least 1 hour, then drained
1/2 cup water (adjust for desired consistency)
1 tbsp nutritional yeast
1/2 tsp smoked paprika
1 clove garlic, minced
Salt and pepper, to taste

For the Zucchini Noodles and Toppings:
4 medium zucchinis, spiralized into noodles
1 tbsp olive oil
1/2 cup tempeh, diced into small cubes
1/2 tsp liquid smoke (optional, for extra smokiness)
Salt and pepper, to taste
Fresh parsley, chopped, for garnish
Freshly cracked black pepper, for garnish

Allergens

CONTAINS SOY   CONTAINS NUTS

INSTRUCTIONS

Prepare the Carbonara Sauce:
In a blender, combine soaked cashews, water, nutritional yeast, smoked paprika, garlic, salt, and pepper. Blend until smooth, adjusting water as needed. Set aside.

Cook the Tempeh "Bacon" Bits:
In a skillet, heat the olive oil over medium heat. Add the diced tempeh and cook for 5-7 minutes, stirring occasionally, until the tempeh becomes golden and crispy.
Add the liquid smoke (if using) and a pinch of salt and pepper to enhance the smoky, "bacon-like" flavor. Continue to cook for another minute, then remove from heat and set aside.

Prepare the Zucchini Noodles:
In the same skillet, add olive oil if needed and sauté the zucchini noodles over medium heat for 2-3 minutes until just tender, being careful not to overcook them as they can release too much water and become soggy. Season with salt and pepper.

Combine and Serve:
Add the cashew carbonara sauce to the skillet with the zucchini noodles, tossing gently to coat evenly. Heat for another 1-2 minutes to warm through.
Plate and top with tempeh "bacon" bits, parsley, and black pepper.

CHEF'S TIPS

Extra Flavor: For a touch more richness, add a dash of white miso paste to the sauce; it will add a subtle depth that resembles the umami of traditional Parmesan.

Variations: If you prefer a more traditional pasta texture, use half zucchini noodles and half cooked spaghetti or linguine.

Tuscan White Bean Soup with Kale

Imagine a steaming bowl of Tuscan White Bean Soup, a rustic Italian classic that's as comforting as it is nourishing. This hearty, vegan soup is a blend of creamy cannellini beans, tender kale, and aromatic herbs, simmered to perfection in a flavorful broth. Each spoonful captures the essence of Tuscany, with its simple, earthy ingredients that come together to create a truly satisfying meal. Perfect for cooler days or as a starter to an Italian-inspired dinner, this soup embodies the warmth and depth of traditional Italian cooking with a plant-based twist.

Wine Pairing: Chianti or a Merlot

Difficulty

 15 min   30 min

INGREDIENTS

4 servings

2 tbsp olive oil

1 yellow onion, finely chopped

2 cloves garlic, minced

2 carrots, diced

2 celery stalks, diced

1 tsp dried rosemary (or 1 fresh sprig)

1 tsp dried thyme

1 bay leaf

4 cups vegetable broth

2 cans (15 oz each) cannellini beans, drained and rinsed

1 bunch kale, stems removed and leaves roughly chopped

Salt and freshly ground black pepper, to taste

Fresh parsley, chopped, for garnish

Crusty bread, for serving

Allergens

INSTRUCTIONS

Sauté the Vegetables
- In a large pot, heat the olive oil over medium heat. Add the chopped onion, garlic, carrots, and celery. Sauté for about 5-7 minutes, stirring occasionally, until the vegetables are softened and fragrant.

Add the Herbs and Broth
- Add the rosemary, thyme, and bay leaf to the pot, stirring to combine with the vegetables. Cook for another minute to let the herbs release their aroma.
- Pour in the vegetable broth and bring the mixture to a gentle boil.

Add the Beans and Kale
- Add the cannellini beans to the pot, stirring well. Reduce the heat to a simmer and let the soup cook for about 15 minutes, allowing the flavors to meld together.
- Add the chopped kale to the pot, stirring it into the soup until it wilts. Cook for another 5 minutes, or until the kale is tender but still vibrant.

Season and Serve
- Season the soup with salt and freshly ground black pepper to taste. Remove the bay leaf before serving.
- Ladle the soup into bowls, garnishing with a sprinkle of fresh parsley. Serve with a side of crusty bread for dipping.

CHEF'S TIPS

Extra Flavour: add a splash of dry white wine after sautéing vegetables and let it reduce before adding broth.

Variation: For a creamier soup, blend a cup of cannellini beans with some broth and mix back into the pot for a thicker texture.

Vegan Butternut Squash Risotto

Golden, creamy, and comforting, this Vegan Butternut Squash Risotto is a celebration of autumnal flavors. Imagine a bowl filled with vibrant orange hues, creamy Arborio rice, and the subtle sweetness of roasted butternut squash, all enhanced by the warmth of sage and a hint of vegan Parmesan. Each bite brings a rich, velvety texture that melts in your mouth, while the aromatic herbs evoke the essence of Italian countryside cooking. This risotto is perfect for cozy evenings or as a show-stopping dish at any gathering, and it pairs beautifully with a crisp white wine.

Wine Pairing: Soave or a Pinot Gris

Difficulty

15 min   35 min

INGREDIENTS

4 servings

2 cups butternut squash, diced into small cubes
2 tbsp olive oil, divided
Salt and freshly ground black pepper, to taste
1 small yellow onion, finely chopped
2 cloves garlic, minced
1 1/2 cups Arborio rice
1/2 cup dry white wine (optional)
4 cups vegetable broth, kept warm
1 tbsp fresh sage, chopped (or 1/2 tsp dried sage)
1/4 cup nutritional yeast or vegan Parmesan
Fresh parsley, chopped, for garnish

Allergens

INSTRUCTIONS

Roast the Butternut Squash
- Preheat oven to 400°F (200°C). Toss diced butternut squash with olive oil, salt, and pepper. Roast on a baking sheet for 20 minutes or until tender, stirring halfway. Set aside.

Sauté the Aromatics
- In a large skillet, heat olive oil over medium. Sauté onion until soft (5-7 minutes), then add garlic for 1 minute until fragrant.

Cook the Rice
- Add Arborio rice, stirring to coat, and toast for 2 minutes. Pour in white wine (if using) and stir until absorbed.

Add the Broth Gradually
- Add warm broth one ladle at a time, stirring until absorbed before adding more.
- Cook for 20-25 minutes until rice is creamy and al dente.

Finish with Butternut Squash and Sage
- Fold in roasted squash and sage, plus nutritional yeast or vegan Parmesan.
- Season, garnish with extra squash, parsley, and vegan Parmesan if desired.

Serve
- Spoon into bowls, garnishing with extra squash, fresh parsley, and vegan Parmesan.

CHEF'S TIPS

Extra Flavor: Add a splash of vegan butter at the end for a richer, silkier finish that enhances the creaminess.

Variations: For added texture, top the risotto with toasted pine nuts or walnuts, which add a nutty crunch that complements the creamy rice.

Spinach and Mushroom Lasagna with Cashew Ricotta

The Spinach and Mushroom Lasagna features layers of lasagna noodles, creamy cashew ricotta, sautéed mushrooms, and spinach, all baked in rich tomato sauce. This hearty dish blends earthy mushroom flavors with sweet spinach, offering a nourishing, dairy-free twist on the Italian classic, ideal for cozy dinners or gatherings.

Wine Pairing: Chianti or a Zinfandel

Difficulty

 25 min   45 min

INGREDIENTS

4 *servings*

For the Cashew Ricotta:
1 1/2 cups raw cashews, soaked for at least 1 hour and drained
1/4 cup water
2 tbsp lemon juice
1 tbsp nutritional yeast
1/2 tsp salt

For the Lasagna:
2 tbsp olive oil
1 large onion, finely chopped
3 cloves garlic, minced
2 cups mushrooms, sliced
4 cups fresh spinach
Salt and black pepper, to taste
3 cups marinara sauce
9 lasagna noodles
Optional: Fresh basil leaves, for garnish

Allergens

 CONTAINS GLUTEN   CONTAINS NUTS

INSTRUCTIONS

Prepare the Cashew Ricotta
- Blend soaked cashews, water, lemon juice, nutritional yeast, and salt until smooth. Adjust water for a ricotta-like texture and season to taste. Set aside.

Sauté the Vegetables
- In a skillet, heat olive oil over medium. Sauté the onion for 5-7 minutes until softened, then add garlic and mushrooms, cooking for another 5-7 minutes until mushrooms release moisture and brown. Add spinach, stirring until wilted (about 2 minutes).Season with salt and pepper, then remove from heat and set aside.

Assemble the Lasagna
- Preheat your oven to 375°F (190°C). In a 9x13-inch baking dish, spread a thin layer of marinara sauce on the bottom.
- Lay three lasagna noodles over the sauce, slightly overlapping them. Spread a third of the cashew ricotta, a third of the spinach and mushroom mixture and a top layer of marinara sauce.Repeat two more times, ending with a final layer of marinara sauce on top.

Bake
- Cover the lasagna with foil and bake in the preheated oven for 25 minutes, then uncover and bake for another 15-20 minutes, or until bubbly and golden on top.

Serve
- Let cool for 5-10 minutes before slicing. Garnish with fresh basil leaves, if desired, and serve warm.

CHEF'S TIPS

Extra Flavor: For a richer taste, add a splash of dry white wine after sautéing vegetables and let it reduce before adding broth

Variations: Sprinkle toasted pine nuts over the cashew ricotta for crunch.

Pasta e Fagioli (Italian Bean and Pasta Soup)

Pasta e Fagioli, or "pasta fazoi," is a comforting Italian-American soup made with tender pasta, creamy cannellini beans, and a rich tomato broth flavored with fresh herbs and garlic. This vegan-friendly dish offers a delightful blend of textures and flavors, ideal for cool evenings or as a hearty lunch, evoking the essence of rustic Italian cooking.

Wine Pairing: Montepulciano d'Abruzzo or a Sangiovese

Difficulty

15 min   30 min

INGREDIENTS

4 servings

2 tbsp olive oil
1 yellow onion, finely chopped
2 cloves garlic, minced
2 carrots, diced
2 celery stalks, diced
1 tsp dried rosemary
1/2 tsp dried thyme
1/4 tsp red pepper flakes
(optional, for a bit of heat)
1 can (14.5 oz) crushed tomatoes
4 cups vegetable broth
1 can (15 oz) cannellini beans,
drained and rinsed
1 cup ditalini or other small pasta
Salt and freshly ground black
pepper, to taste
Fresh parsley, chopped, for
garnish
Vegan Parmesan cheese, for
garnish (optional)

Allergens

CONTAINS
GLUTEN

INSTRUCTIONS

Sauté the Aromatics
- In a large pot, heat olive oil over medium, then sauté onion, carrots, and celery for 5-7 minutes until softened.
- Add the minced garlic, rosemary, thyme, and red pepper flakes (if using). Cook for an additional minute until fragrant.

Build the Broth
- Stir in the crushed tomatoes and vegetable broth. Bring the mixture to a boil, then reduce the heat to a simmer.

Add the Beans and Pasta
- Add the cannellini beans to the pot and let the soup simmer for 10 minutes to allow the flavors to meld together.
- Add the pasta and cook per package instructions (usually about 8-10 minutes), stirring occasionally to prevent sticking.

Season and Serve
- Taste the soup and adjust seasoning with salt and black pepper as needed.
- Ladle the soup into bowls and garnish with chopped fresh parsley and a sprinkle of vegan Parmesan if desired. Serve hot.

CHEF'S TIPS

Extra Flavor: Add a splash of red wine to the pot after the vegetables have softened to enhance the depth of the broth.

Variations: For a creamier texture, blend a small portion of the beans with a bit of broth and stir back into the pot. This will give the soup a thicker, richer consistency.

Spaghetti Aglio, Olio e Peperoncino

Spaghetti Aglio e Olio e Peperoncino is a true Italian classic that embodies the elegance of simplicity. With only a handful of ingredients—garlic, olive oil, chili, and pasta—this dish transforms into a symphony of flavors. The garlic becomes fragrant and slightly caramelized, infusing the olive oil with its rich aroma, while the peperoncino adds a gentle heat that complements the nuttiness of the pasta. This vegan pasta is perfect for those who appreciate bold flavors and refined textures, making it a versatile and satisfying meal for any occasion.

Wine Pairing: Verdicchio or a Sauvignon Blanc

Difficulty

5 min   10 min

INGREDIENTS

4 servings

12 oz spaghetti
1/3 cup extra virgin olive oil
6 cloves garlic, thinly sliced
1 tsp red pepper flakes (adjust to taste)
Salt, to taste
Freshly ground black pepper, to taste
Fresh parsley, chopped, for garnish (optional)
Lemon zest, for garnish (optional)

Allergens

CONTAINS
GLUTEN

INSTRUCTIONS

Cook the Spaghetti

- Bring a large pot of salted water to a boil. Add the spaghetti and cook according to package instructions until al dente. Reserve 1/2 cup of pasta water, then drain the pasta.

Prepare the Aglio e Olio Sauce

- While the pasta is cooking, heat the olive oil in a large skillet over medium-low heat. Add the sliced garlic, stirring occasionally, and cook until it begins to turn golden brown, about 2-3 minutes. Be careful not to burn the garlic, as it can become bitter.
- Add the red pepper flakes to the oil and sauté for another 30 seconds, allowing the chili to infuse into the oil.

Combine Pasta and Sauce

- Add the cooked spaghetti directly into the skillet with the garlic and chili oil. Toss to coat the pasta in the oil mixture, adding a bit of reserved pasta water as needed to help the sauce adhere to the noodles.

Season and Serve

- Season the pasta with salt and freshly ground black pepper to taste. Divide the spaghetti among plates and garnish with chopped fresh parsley and a sprinkle of lemon zest if desired.

CHEF'S TIPS

Extra Flavor: For a burst of flavor, add a few halved cherry tomatoes to the oil along with the garlic. This will add a subtle sweetness that balances the spiciness of the peperoncino.

Variations: For a creamier texture, stir in a tablespoon of vegan butter at the end.

Vegan Pumpkin Gnocchi with Brown Butter Sage Sauce

Vegan Pumpkin Gnocchi features soft, pillowy dumplings with subtle pumpkin sweetness, dressed in fragrant brown butter sage sauce. This dish brings autumn's warm colors and flavors to your table, combining unique creaminess with earthy undertones. Each bite offers a comforting yet elegant taste of Italian tradition, perfect for cozy dinners or festive gatherings.

Wine Pairing: Pinot Grigio or a Chardonnay

Difficulty

 30 min   10 min

INGREDIENTS

4 servings

For the Pumpkin Gnocchi:
1 cup canned pumpkin puree (not pumpkin pie filling)
1 cup all-purpose flour (plus more for dusting)
1/4 cup potato starch or cornstarch
1/2 tsp salt
1/4 tsp nutmeg (optional, for a hint of warmth)

For the Brown Butter Sage Sauce:
1/4 cup vegan butter
8-10 fresh sage leaves
Salt and freshly ground black pepper, to taste
2 tbsp nutritional yeast (optional, for a "cheesy" note)
Pumpkin seeds, toasted, for garnish (optional)

Allergens

CONTAINS GLUTEN

INSTRUCTIONS

Make the Dough
- Mix pumpkin puree, flour, potato starch (or cornstarch), salt, and nutmeg in a bowl until a soft, slightly sticky dough forms. Knead on a floured surface until smooth.
- Add a little extra flour if necessary, until it becomes smooth and only slightly tacky.

Shape the Gnocchi
- Divide dough into four portions, roll into 1/2-inch ropes, and cut into 1-inch pieces. Optionally, roll each piece on a fork for ridges, which help the sauce cling to the gnocchi.

Cook the Gnocchi
Boil salted water and cook gnocchi in batches. They're done when they float (about 2-3 minutes). Remove with a slotted spoon and drain and transfer them to a plate lined with paper towels to drain any excess water.

Prepare the Sauce
• In a skillet, melt vegan butter over medium heat. Add sage leaves, cooking until butter browns and sage crisps (2-3 minutes). Season with salt, pepper, and nutritional yeast if desired, stirring to combine.

Toss and Serve and serve
Add gnocchi to the skillet, tossing to coat. Cook for an additional minute to let the flavors meld.Serve garnished with crispy sage and toasted pumpkin seeds. Serve warm.

CHEF'S TIPS

Extra Flavor: For an added layer of richness, stir a small amount of truffle oil into the sauce just before serving to complement the earthy sage and pumpkin.

Variations: You can replace pumpkin puree with sweet potato or butternut squash for a slightly different flavor profile.

Farfalle al Pesto di Spinaci (Bowtie Pasta with Spinach Pesto)

Farfalle al Pesto di Spinaci features vibrant green pesto on bowtie pasta, combining tender baby spinach, basil, and garlic for a fresh twist on traditional pesto. The creamy, vegan sauce enhances the sweetness of spinach and brightness of lemon, complementing the al dente pasta. This light yet satisfying dish is easy to prepare and adds color and flavor to any meal, making it suitable for all seasons.

Wine Pairing: Vermentino or a Sauvignon Blanc

Difficulty

10 min   10 min

INGREDIENTS

4 servings

For the Spinach Pesto:
4 cups baby spinach leaves
1/2 cup fresh basil leaves
1/3 cup raw cashews or walnuts (soaked in warm water for 10 minutes, then drained)
2 cloves garlic, minced
1/4 cup nutritional yeast
Zest and juice of 1 lemon
1/4 cup extra virgin olive oil
Salt and freshly ground black pepper, to taste

For the Pasta:
12 oz farfalle (bowtie pasta)
Salt, for pasta water
Fresh cherry tomatoes, halved, for garnish (optional)
Vegan Parmesan cheese, for garnish (optional)

Allergens

CONTAINS
GLUTEN

CONTAINS
NUTS

INSTRUCTIONS

Cook the Pasta
Bring a large pot of salted water to a boil. Add the farfalle and cook according to package instructions until al dente, usually about 10 minutes.
Reserve 1/2 cup of pasta cooking water before draining, as it can help adjust the pesto consistency later.

Prepare the Spinach Pesto
In a food processor, blend spinach, basil, nuts, garlic, nutritional yeast, lemon zest, and juice. Gradually add olive oil until smooth, using pasta water if needed. Season with salt and pepper.

Combine the Pasta and Pesto
Toss farfalle with pesto, adding reserved water if needed for a smooth coating.

Serve
Divide into bowls, garnish with cherry tomatoes and vegan Parmesan if desired. Buon appetito!

CHEF'S TIPS

Extra Flavor: For an added touch of creaminess, blend in a small avocado with the spinach pesto. It adds a luxurious texture and a hint of richness that complements the spinach beautifully.

Variations: You can substitute spinach with arugula for a slightly peppery twist, or add sun-dried tomatoes to the pesto for a sweet, tangy flavor.

Minestrone alla Genovese

Minestrone alla Genovese is a vibrant vegan soup filled with fresh seasonal vegetables, creamy beans, and al dente pasta, all in a savory broth. Infused with basil from pesto, it captures the essence of an Italian garden and offers a healthy, comforting meal.

Wine Pairing: **Ligurian Vermentino or a Chardonnay**

Difficulty

5 min   10 min

INGREDIENTS

4 servings

For the Soup:
2 tbsp olive oil
1 onion, finely chopped
2 cloves garlic, minced
1 large carrot, diced
1 celery stalk, diced
1 zucchini, diced
1 medium potato, peeled and diced
1/2 cup green beans, trimmed and
cut into 1-inch pieces
1 can (14 oz) diced tomatoes
4 cups vegetable broth
1 can (15 oz) cannellini beans,
drained and rinsed
1/2 cup small pasta (such as
ditalini or small shells)
Salt and freshly ground black
pepper, to taste

For the Basil Pesto:
2 cups fresh basil leaves
1/4 cup raw pine nuts or walnuts
1/4 cup nutritional yeast
1/4 cup extra virgin olive oil
1 clove garlic, minced
Salt and pepper, to taste

Allergens

CONTAINS   CONTAINS
GLUTEN   NUTS

INSTRUCTIONS

Sauté the Aromatics

- Heat olive oil in a large pot over medium. Sauté onion, garlic, carrot, and celery for 5-7 minutes until softened and fragrant.

Add the Vegetables and Broth

- Add the diced zucchini, potato, green beans, and canned tomatoes to the pot, stirring to combine with the sautéed vegetables.
- Pour them in the broth, bring to a boil, then reduce to a simmer. Cover and cook for 15 minutes, or until the potatoes are tender.

Add the Beans and Pasta

- Stir in the cannellini beans and pasta, and season with salt and pepper. Continue simmering for another 8-10 minutes, or until the pasta is al dente. Stir occasionally to prevent the pasta from sticking.

Prepare the Basil Pesto

- While the soup is simmering, blend basil leaves, pine nuts, nutritional yeast, olive oil, and minced garlic. Blend until smooth, adding a touch more oil if needed to achieve a creamy consistency.
- Season with salt and pepper to taste, then set aside.

Serve the Soup

Ladle soup into bowls and top with a spoonful of pesto, swirling just before eating to enjoy the full aroma and flavor.

CHEF'S TIPS

Extra Flavor: For an added depth of flavor, add a small piece of Vegan Parmesan rind to the soup while it simmers, then remove before serving.

Variations: Substitute or add other seasonal vegetables, such as spinach, cabbage, or peas, to the minestrone.

Pappardelle with Wild Mushroom Ragù

Imagine wide ribbons of pappardelle pasta combined with a rich wild mushroom ragù, celebrating umami flavors. Various mushrooms simmered with garlic, herbs, and red wine create a deeply satisfying vegan sauce. This dish captures the essence of the Italian countryside, offering hearty yet elegant comfort food perfect for cozy evenings or special occasions.

Wine Pairing: Chianti or a Pinot Noir

Difficulty

15 min   30 min

INGREDIENTS

4 servings

For the Mushroom Ragù:

2 tbsp olive oil

1 large onion, finely chopped

3 cloves garlic, minced

1 lb mixed wild mushrooms (such as cremini, shiitake, oyster, or porcini), sliced

1/2 cup dry red wine

1 can (14.5 oz) diced tomatoes

1/2 cup vegetable broth

1 tsp dried thyme

1 tsp dried rosemary

Salt and freshly ground black pepper, to taste

Fresh parsley, chopped, for garnish

For the Pasta:

12 oz pappardelle pasta

Salt, for pasta water

Olive oil, for drizzling (optional)

Allergens

CONTAINS GLUTEN

INSTRUCTIONS

Prepare the Mushroom Ragù

- In a skillet, heat olive oil over medium ,sauté chopped onion for 5-7 minutes until softened and golden.
- Add the minced garlic and sliced mushrooms. Sauté for another 5-7 minutes, stirring occasionally, until the mushrooms release their moisture and begin to brown.

Deglaze with Wine and Build the Sauce

- Pour the red wine into the skillet, stirring to deglaze and lift any caramelized bits from the bottom. Let the wine simmer for 2-3 minutes until slightly reduced.
- Add the diced tomatoes, vegetable broth, thyme, and rosemary. Season with salt and pepper. Simmer and cook for 15 minutes until the sauce thickens and the flavors meld together.

Cook the Pappardelle

- While the sauce simmers, boil salted water, add the pappardelle and cook until al dente, about 8-10 minutes. Reserve 1/4 cup of pasta cooking water.

Combine the Pasta and Ragù and serve

- Add the drained pappardelle with the mushroom ragù, tossing gently to coat the pasta in the sauce. Add a bit of pasta water if needed.
- Divide the pappardelle among plates, garnish with freshly chopped parsley, and serve hot.

CHEF'S TIPS

Extra Flavor: Add a teaspoon of balsamic vinegar to the ragù at the end of cooking for a touch of acidity that enhances the earthy flavors of the mushrooms.

Variations: For an added layer of texture, mix in some chopped walnuts or toasted pine nuts when serving, bringing a nutty crunch that complements the soft mushrooms.

03

Secondi Piatti (Main Courses)

Overview

In Italian cuisine, "**secondi piatti**" (second courses) are typically the main protein-centered dishes that follow the pasta or soup course (primo piatto). For plant-based Italian cooking, secondi focus on hearty vegetables, legumes, and plant proteins prepared with flavorful herbs, sauces, and seasonings that bring out the essence of Italian tradition. Examples include dishes like eggplant-based melanzane alla parmigiana, vegetable-stuffed peppers, or rich mushroom and lentil ragùs. These plant-based secondi capture the comforting, robust flavors of Italian cooking in a way that's satisfying and nourishing.

Explore more secondi piatti recipes at *FreshPlantBased.com*!

Eggplant Involtini Stuffed with Cashew Ricotta

Eggplant Involtini is a delightful Italian dish featuring thin, roasted eggplant slices rolled with a creamy cashew ricotta filling. Topped with warm tomato sauce and fresh herbs, this vegan dish balances creaminess and acidity. Ideal as a main course or appetizer, it elegantly showcases Italian cuisine in a plant-based form.

Wine Pairing: Sangiovese or a Merlot

Difficulty

25 min   12 min

INGREDIENTS

4 servings

For the Cashew Ricotta:
1 1/2 cups raw cashews, soaked for at least 2 hours, then drained
1/4 cup water
2 tbsp lemon juice
1 clove garlic, minced
1/4 cup nutritional yeast
Salt and freshly ground black pepper, to taste
2 tbsp fresh basil, chopped

For the Eggplant Rolls:
2 medium eggplants, sliced lengthwise into 1/4-inch thick strips
Salt, for sprinkling
2 tbsp olive oil

For the Tomato Sauce:
1 tbsp olive oil
1 small onion, finely chopped
2 cloves garlic, minced
1 can (14.5 oz) crushed tomatoes
1 tsp dried oregano
Salt and freshly ground black pepper, to taste
Fresh basil leaves, for garnish

Allergens

CONTAINS NUTS

INSTRUCTIONS

Prepare the Cashew Ricotta
- Blend soaked cashews, water, lemon juice, garlic, nutritional yeast, salt, and pepper until smooth and creamy.
- Stir in the chopped basil and adjust seasoning. Set aside.

Prepare the Eggplant
- Preheat oven to 400°F (200°C). Salt eggplant slices and let sit for 10 minutes, then pat dry. Brush with olive oil and roast for 15 minutes until tender and pliable but not mushy.

Prepare the Tomato Sauce
- While the eggplant is roasting, add the chopped onion in a saucepan with 1tbs olive oil and sauté for 5 minutes until softened.
- Add the minced garlic and cook for another minute, stir in the crushed tomatoes and oregano. Season with salt and pepper. Simmer for 10-15 minutes until the sauce thickens slightly.

Assemble the Involtini
- Spread tomato sauce in a baking dish. Place a spoonful of ricotta on each eggplant slice at one end, and roll to form a neat roll. Place the roll seam-side down in the baking dish. Repeat with the remaining eggplant slices.

Bake
- Cover with remaining sauce, cover with foil, and bake for 20 minutes. Remove foil and bake 10 more minutes until bubbly and golden.

Serve
- Garnish with fresh basil leaves and serve warm, with a drizzle of olive oil if desired.

CHEF'S TIPS

Extra Flavor: Add red pepper flakes to the sauce for subtle heat.

Variations: For a heartier meal, add a layer of cooked quinoa or sautéed spinach to the filling. It adds texture and a bit of extra nutrition.

Chickpea and Mushroom Ragù over Polenta

Picture a cozy bowl of creamy polenta crowned with a delicious chickpea and mushroom ragù. This delightful vegan dish showcases earthy mushrooms and robust chickpeas simmered in a rich, flavorful sauce infused with garlic, rosemary, and red wine. The ragù's rich umami flavors beautifully contrast with the silky polenta, creating a comforting yet sophisticated option for intimate dinners, truly capturing the essence of rustic Italian cuisine.

Wine Pairing: Barbera or a Zinfandel

Difficulty

15 min   30 min

INGREDIENTS

4 servings

For the Mushroom and Chickpea Ragù:

2 tbsp olive oil
1 small onion, finely chopped
3 cloves garlic, minced
2 cups mushrooms (such as cremini or portobello), chopped
1 can (15 oz) chickpeas, drained and rinsed
1/2 cup dry red wine
1 can (14.5 oz) crushed tomatoes
1 tsp dried rosemary
1 tsp dried thyme
Salt and freshly ground black pepper, to taste
Fresh parsley, chopped, for garnish

For the Polenta:

1 cup polenta (coarse cornmeal)
4 cups water or vegetable broth
1 tbsp olive oil or vegan butter
Salt, to taste

Allergens

INSTRUCTIONS

Prepare the Mushroom and Chickpea Ragù

- Heat olive oil in a skillet over medium, sauté onion for 5 minutes, then add garlic for 1 minute. Stir in mushrooms and cook until browned, about 5-7 minutes until they release their moisture and start to brown.

Add the Wine and Tomatoes

- Pour in red wine, simmer for 2-3 minutes until it reduces slightly.
- Add chickpeas, tomatoes, rosemary, thyme, salt, and pepper. Simmer for 15-20 minutes until thickened.

Prepare the Polenta

- While the ragù is simmering, boil 4 cups of water or broth, add salt.
- Slowly whisk in the polenta, reducing the heat to low. Stir frequently to prevent lumps from forming.
- Continue cooking the polenta for 20 minutes, or until it reaches a smooth, creamy consistency. Stir in olive oil or vegan butter, adjusting salt.

Serve

- Spoon a generous portion of polenta into each bowl. Top with the chickpea and mushroom ragù, garnishing with chopped fresh parsley. Serve warm.

CHEF'S TIPS

Extra Flavor: For a smoky touch, add a pinch of smoked paprika to the ragù. It enhances the depth and complements the earthy mushrooms and chickpeas beautifully.

Variations: For added richness, stir in a bit of nutritional yeast or vegan Parmesan into the polenta before serving.

Tofu Piccata with Lemon-Caper Sauce

Tofu Piccata offers a refreshing twist on an Italian classic with crispy tofu cutlets in a zesty lemon-caper sauce. The tofu absorbs the sauce's vibrant flavors, complemented by fresh parsley for added freshness. This light and elegant dish is easy to prepare, perfect for weeknight dinners or impressing guests.

Wine Pairing: Pinot Grigio or a Sauvignon Blanc

Difficulty

15 min   20 min

INGREDIENTS

4 servings

For the Tofu Piccata:
1 lb firm tofu, pressed and sliced into 1/2-inch thick cutlets
Salt and freshly ground black pepper, to taste
1/2 cup all-purpose flour (or gluten-free flour, if preferred)
2 tbsp olive oil

For the Lemon-Caper Sauce:
1 tbsp olive oil
2 cloves garlic, minced
1/2 cup vegetable broth
1/4 cup dry white wine (optional)
1/4 cup freshly squeezed lemon juice
2 tbsp capers, drained
Salt and black pepper, to taste
Fresh parsley, chopped, for garnish

Allergens

CONTAINS
SOY

INSTRUCTIONS

Prepare the Tofu Cutlets
- Season the tofu cutlets with salt and pepper. Dredge each cutlet in flour, shaking off any excess, to give a light coating.

Sear the Tofu
- Heat 2 tablespoons of olive oil in a large skillet over medium-high heat. Once hot, add the tofu cutlets in a single layer. Sear each side for about 3-4 minutes, or until golden brown and crispy.
- Remove the tofu from the skillet and set aside on a plate while you prepare the sauce.

Make the Lemon-Caper Sauce
- In the same skillet, add 1 tablespoon of olive oil and the minced garlic. Sauté for 1 minute, until the garlic is fragrant but not browned.
- Pour in the vegetable broth, white wine (if using), and lemon juice. Stir in the capers, then season with a pinch of salt and black pepper. Bring the sauce to a simmer and cook for 3-4 minutes, allowing it to reduce slightly and the flavors to meld.

Return the Tofu to the Skillet
- Place the tofu cutlets back in the skillet with the sauce, spooning some of the sauce over each piece to coat. Let the tofu simmer in the sauce for another 2-3 minutes to absorb the flavors.

Serve
- Transfer the tofu cutlets to a serving plate, spooning extra lemon-caper sauce over the top. Garnish with fresh parsley for a pop of color and freshness. Serve warm.

CHEF'S TIPS

Extra Flavor: Add a dash of vegan butter to the sauce at the end of cooking for a richer, creamier finish.

Variations: For added texture, coat the tofu cutlets in panko breadcrumbs before searing, creating an extra-crispy crust.

Vegan Osso Buco with Jackfruit

Imagine a savory stew with tender jackfruit in a rich tomato and vegetable sauce, flavored with rosemary and thyme. This Vegan Osso Buco is a plant-based version of the classic dish, where jackfruit mimics texture and absorbs flavors. Carrots, celery, and onions form a flavorful base, ideal for cozy dinners or special occasions.

Wine Pairing: Chianti or a Merlot

Difficulty

◆ ◆ ◆

20 min   45 min

INGREDIENTS

4 servings

For the Osso Buco:
2 tbsp olive oil
1 large onion, finely chopped
2 carrots, diced
2 celery stalks, diced
3 cloves garlic, minced
1 lb young green jackfruit
(canned or fresh), drained and
pulled apart into pieces
1/2 cup dry white wine (optional)
1 can (14.5 oz) diced tomatoes
1/2 cup vegetable broth
1 tbsp tomato paste
1 tsp dried thyme
1 tsp dried rosemary
Salt and freshly ground black
pepper, to taste
Fresh parsley, chopped, for
garnish

For the Gremolata (optional but recommended):
Zest of 1 lemon
1 clove garlic, minced
2 tbsp fresh parsley, finely
chopped

Allergens

INSTRUCTIONS

Prepare the Base
- In a skillet, heat olive oil over medium, add onion, carrots, and celery, cooking 5-7 minutes until softened.
- Add garlic for another minute until fragrant.

Add the Jackfruit
- Add the jackfruit pieces to the skillet and cook for 3-4 minutes to let the jackfruit absorb some flavor.

Deglaze and Build the Sauce
- Pour in the white wine (if using), stirring well to deglaze the pan and lift any caramelized bits from the bottom. Let the wine simmer for 2-3 minutes until it reduces slightly.
- Add tomatoes, broth, tomato paste, thyme, rosemary, salt, and pepper combining everything well.

Simmer the Osso Buco
- Reduce the heat to low, cover the skillet or Dutch oven, and let the mixture simmer for 30-35 minutes. Stir occasionally, adding a little more vegetable broth if needed to maintain a thick but pourable consistency. The jackfruit should become tender and pull apart easily.

Prepare the Gremolata
- While the osso buco simmers, make the gremolata by combining the lemon zest, minced garlic, and chopped parsley in a small bowl. This fresh topping adds brightness to the dish.

Serve
- Spoon the jackfruit osso buco onto plates or bowls, topping each portion with a sprinkle of gremolata for extra flavor and garnish with fresh parsley.

CHEF'S TIPS

Extra Flavor: For a more intense flavor, add a dash of balsamic vinegar to the sauce just before serving to enhance the tomato and herb flavors.

Variations: Substitute the jackfruit with king oyster mushrooms or seitan for a different texture, or add sliced green olives for a briny contrast.

Stuffed Bell Peppers with Italian Herbs and Quinoa

Picture this: vibrant bell peppers bursting with a scrumptious blend of fluffy quinoa, zesty Italian herbs, and juicy cherry tomatoes! Each pepper is like a tasty treasure chest, crammed with flavor as the quinoa soaks up all that deliciousness while the peppers bring a sweet kick. These Stuffed Bell Peppers with Italian Herbs and Quinoa are the ultimate hearty, healthy plant-based feast!

Wine Pairing: Pinot Grigio or a Chardonnay

Difficulty

15 min   30 min

INGREDIENTS

4 servings

4 large bell peppers (red, yellow, or orange), tops sliced off and seeds removed
1 cup quinoa, rinsed
2 cups vegetable broth
1 tbsp olive oil
1 small onion, finely chopped
2 cloves garlic, minced
1 cup cherry tomatoes, halved
1/2 cup zucchini, diced
1 tsp dried oregano
1 tsp dried basil
Salt and freshly ground black pepper, to taste
Fresh parsley, chopped, for garnish

Allergens

INSTRUCTIONS

Prepare the Quinoa Filling
- In a saucepan boil vegetables broth. Add quinoa, reduce the heat to low, cover, and let it simmer for 15 minutes, or until absorbed. Fluff and set aside.

Sauté the Vegetables
- In skillet, heat the olive oil over medium heat. Add onion and sauté for 5 minutes, until softened.
- Add the garlic, cherry tomatoes, and diced zucchini. Cook for another 5 minutes until the tomatoes soften.

Combine with Quinoa and Seasonings
- In the skillet mix quinoa with the sautéed vegetables, oregano, basil, salt, and black pepper. Adjust seasoning.

Stuff the Bell Peppers
- Preheat your oven to 375°F (190°C). Arrange the bell peppers in a baking dish, standing upright. Fill bell peppers with quinoa mixture.

Bake the Stuffed Peppers
- Cover with foil and bake for 20 minutes. Uncover and bake 10 more minutes until peppers are tender but still hold their shape.

Serve
- Garnish the stuffed peppers with fresh parsley and serve warm.

CHEF'S TIPS

Extra Flavor: Sprinkle a bit of vegan Parmesan on top of each pepper before baking for an added layer of savory richness.

Variations: Add black olives or artichoke hearts to the quinoa mixture for a Mediterranean twist, or use farro or couscous instead of quinoa for a different texture.

Vegan Sausage and Peppers

Vegan Sausage and Peppers is a vibrant and hearty dish inspired by Italian street food. It features seared plant-based sausage and colorful bell peppers sautéed with onions, garlic, and Italian herbs for a flavorful meal. Quick and easy to prepare, it's perfect for weeknight dinners or casual gatherings, served on a baguette or over pasta.

Wine Pairing: Montepulciano d'Abruzzo or a Zinfandel

Difficulty

10 min   20 min

INGREDIENTS

4 servings

For the Sausage and Peppers:
2 tbsp olive oil
4 vegan sausages, sliced
diagonally into 1/2-inch pieces
1 large onion, sliced
1 red bell pepper, sliced
1 yellow bell pepper, sliced
1 green bell pepper, sliced
3 cloves garlic, minced
1/2 tsp dried oregano
1/2 tsp dried basil
Salt and freshly ground black
pepper, to taste
Fresh parsley, chopped, for
garnish

For Serving (optional):
Crusty baguette or hoagie rolls
Cooked pasta or rice

Allergens

**CONTAINS
GLUTEN**

INSTRUCTIONS

Sear the Vegan Sausages

- In a large skillet, heat 1 tablespoon of olive oil over medium heat. Add the sliced vegan sausage and cook for 3-4 minutes on each side, or until golden and crispy. Remove the sausages from the skillet and set aside.

Sauté the Vegetables

- In the same skillet, add the remaining 1 tablespoon of olive oil. Add the sliced onion and cook for 3-4 minutes, stirring occasionally, until it begins to soften.
- Add the red, yellow, and green bell peppers to the skillet. Sauté for another 5 minutes, or until the peppers start to soften and develop a slight char.

Add Garlic and Seasonings

- Add the minced garlic, oregano, and basil to the skillet. Stir and cook for 1-2 minutes, allowing the garlic and herbs to release their fragrance.
- Season with salt and black pepper to taste.

Combine and Serve

- Return the cooked vegan sausage to the skillet, stirring to combine with the vegetables. Cook for another 2-3 minutes to allow the flavors to meld.
- Garnish with fresh parsley and serve hot.

Serve Options

- Serve the sausage and peppers over pasta or rice, or pile them onto a crusty baguette or hoagie roll for a delicious Italian sandwich.

CHEF'S TIPS

Extra Flavor: For added depth, add balsamic vinegar or vegan Worcestershire sauce to enhance caramelization and acidity.

Variations: Add sliced mushrooms for a meatier texture, or crushed red pepper flakes for a hint of spice. Alternatively, stir in some marinara sauce for a saucier version.

Portobello Mushroom Marsala

Portobello Mushroom Marsala is an elegant dish featuring meaty portobello mushrooms in a rich Marsala wine sauce with garlic, thyme, and rosemary. The sauce enhances the mushrooms' umami flavors, while fresh parsley adds brightness. It's perfect as a main course over creamy polenta or mashed potatoes, ideal for cozy dinners or special occasions with classic Italian flavors.

Wine Pairing: Chianti or a Pinot Noir

Difficulty

10 min   20 min

INGREDIENTS

4 servings

4 large portobello mushrooms, cleaned and thickly sliced
2 tbsp olive oil
1 small onion, finely chopped
3 cloves garlic, minced
1/2 cup Marsala wine (or substitute with 1/2 cup dry sherry or a mix of vegetable broth and a splash of balsamic vinegar)
3/4 cup vegetable broth
1 tsp fresh thyme (or 1/2 tsp dried thyme)
1/2 tsp dried rosemary
Salt and freshly ground black pepper, to taste
Fresh parsley, chopped, for garnish

Allergens

INSTRUCTIONS

Prepare the Mushrooms

- In a skillet, heat 1 tbs of olive oil over medium-high heat.
- Add the sliced portobello mushrooms in a single layer and cook for 4-5 minutes, flipping once halfway through, until they're golden brown and slightly caramelized. Remove and set aside.

Sauté the Onion and Garlic

- In the same skillet, add the remaining tablespoon of olive oil. Add onion and cook for 3-4 minutes, then add garlic and cook for an additional minute.

Deglaze with Marsala and Add Herbs

- Pour in Marsala to deglaze, simmer for 2-3 mins.
- Add the vegetable broth, thyme, and rosemary. Stir well to combine.

Simmer the Sauce

- Return mushrooms, simmer for 5-7 mins until sauce thickens and the mushrooms absorb its flavor. Season to taste.

Serve

- Transfer the Portobello Mushroom Marsala to plates, garnishing with freshly chopped parsley. Serve warm over creamy polenta, mashed potatoes, or pasta.

CHEF'S TIPS

Extra Flavor: Add a splash of balsamic vinegar or a teaspoon of Dijon mustard to the sauce for a deeper, more complex flavor that balances the Marsala's sweetness.

Variations: If you can't find Marsala wine, substitute with a dry sherry or a mixture of vegetable broth and a dash of balsamic vinegar for a similar depth and slight sweetness.

Lentil Bolognese with Rigatoni

Lentil Bolognese is a hearty, vegan alternative to traditional Italian Bolognese. It features a thick tomato sauce filled with tender lentils, garlic, and fresh herbs, offering a rich flavor and robust texture. Nutritious and filling, the lentils provide an earthy bite that complements the sweetness of the tomatoes, making it a comforting dish to enjoy.

Wine Pairing: Chianti or a Cabernet Sauvignon

Difficulty

10 min   30 min

INGREDIENTS

4 servings

For the Lentil Bolognese:
2 tbsp olive oil
1 large onion, finely chopped
2 cloves garlic, minced
1 large carrot, diced
1 celery stalk, diced
1 cup dried green or brown lentils, rinsed
1 can (14.5 oz) crushed tomatoes
3 cups vegetable broth
2 tbsp tomato paste
1 tsp dried basil
1 tsp dried oregano
1/2 tsp dried thyme
Salt and freshly ground black pepper, to taste
Fresh parsley, chopped, for garnish

For the Pasta:
12 oz rigatoni pasta
Salt, for pasta water

Allergens

CONTAINS GLUTEN

INSTRUCTIONS

Sauté the Vegetables
- In a skillet, heat the olive oil over medium heat. Add the onion, carrot, and celery, and sauté for about 5-7 minutes, until softened and golden.
- Add garlic and cook for 1 minute until fragrant.

Add the Lentils and Tomato Base
- Stir in the rinsed lentils, tomato paste, and crushed tomatoes, combining everything well.
- Add the vegetable broth, basil, oregano, and thyme. Stir to mix, then bring the sauce to a gentle simmer.

Simmer the Bolognese Sauce
- Reduce the heat to low, cover, simmer for 25-30 minutes, until lentils are tender. Stir occasionally and season to taste.

Cook the Rigatoni
- While the Bolognese sauce is simmering, bring a pot of salted water to a boil. Add the rigatoni and cook according to package instructions until al dente, about 10 minutes.
- Drain the pasta, reserving a little of the pasta water.

Combine the Pasta and Sauce
- Add the cooked rigatoni to the skillet with the Lentil Bolognese, tossing to coat the pasta with the sauce. Add pasta water if needed to help the sauce adhere to the rigatoni.

Serve
- Divide the Lentil Bolognese over Rigatoni onto plates, garnishing with freshly chopped parsley. Serve hot.

CHEF'S TIPS

Extra Flavor: For added depth, stir in a splash of balsamic vinegar or a pinch of red pepper flakes for a subtle heat at the end of cooking.

Variations: Swap the rigatoni for other pasta shapes like spaghetti, pappardelle, or penne. For a grain-free option, serve the Bolognese over zucchini noodles or spaghetti squash.

Vegan Parmigiana di Melanzane (Eggplant Parmesan)

Vegan Parmigiana di Melanzane is a delightful plant-based version of the Italian classic. It features layers of golden-fried eggplant, rich tomato sauce, and creamy dairy-free mozzarella, baked until bubbly. This dish combines earthy eggplant, bright tomato acidity, and comforting vegan cheese, making it ideal for family dinners or special occasions.

Wine Pairing: Sangiovese or a Pinot Noir

Difficulty

20 min · 40 min

INGREDIENTS

4 servings

For the Eggplant:

2 large eggplants, sliced into 1/4-inch rounds

Salt, for sweating the eggplant

1 cup all-purpose flour (or gluten-free flour, if needed)

1 cup unsweetened plant milk

1 cup breadcrumbs (use gluten-free breadcrumbs if needed)

1/2 tsp dried oregano

1/2 tsp dried basil

Olive oil, for frying

For the Tomato Sauce:

2 tbsp olive oil

1 small onion, finely chopped

2 cloves garlic, minced

1 can (14.5 oz) crushed tomatoes

1 tsp dried oregano

Salt and freshly ground black pepper, to taste

Fresh basil leaves, torn, for garnish

For Assembly:

1 cup vegan mozzarella cheese, shredded

Fresh basil leaves, for garnish

Allergens

CONTAINS GLUTEN · CONTAINS NUTS

INSTRUCTIONS

Prepare the Eggplant

- Place the eggplant slices on a tray and sprinkle each side with a generous pinch of salt. Let the eggplant sit for 15 minutes to sweat out any bitterness then pat dry.

Bread the Eggplant

- Place the flour in one bowl, the plant milk in another, and mix the breadcrumbs with the oregano and basil in a third bowl.
- Dip each eggplant slice first in the flour, then in the plant milk, and finally in the breadcrumb mixture, pressing gently to adhere.

Fry the Eggplant

- In a skillet, heat a thin layer of olive oil over medium heat. Fry the eggplant slices in batches for 2-3 minutes per side until golden and then drain on paper towel.

Prepare the Tomato Sauce

- In a saucepan, heat 2 tablespoons of olive oil over medium heat. Add onion and sauté for 5 minutes until softened.
- Add the garlic and cook for one minute until fragrant, then add the tomatoes, oregano, salt and pepper. Simmer for 10 minutes until the sauce thickens.

Assemble the Parmigiana

- Preheat oven to 375°F (190°C). In a baking dish, spread a thin layer of tomato sauce on the bottom.
- Place a layer of fried eggplant slices on top, followed by a sprinkle of vegan mozzarella. Repeat the layers, finishing with a generous layer of sauce and a final sprinkle of vegan mozzarella on top.

Bake

- Cover with foil and bake for 20 minutes. Uncover and bake 10 more minutes until the cheese is melted and bubbly.

Serve

- Garnish with fresh basil leaves and serve warm.

CHEF'S TIPS

Extra Flavor: Add a drizzle of balsamic reduction over the top before serving for a touch of sweetness that complements the tomato and basil.

Variations: For a healthier twist, you can bake the breaded eggplant slices at 400°F (200°C) for 15 minutes, flipping halfway through, instead of frying them.

Stuffed Zucchini Boats with Cashew Parmesan

Imagine vibrant green zucchini boats filled with a savory mixture of fresh vegetables and topped with golden cashew Parmesan. These Stuffed Zucchini Boats are visually appealing and flavorful, featuring tender zucchini, juicy tomatoes, and protein-rich chickpeas, complemented by a cheesy, crunchy finish. This dish is perfect for satisfying meals.

Wine Pairing: Vermentino or a Sauvignon Blanc

Difficulty

15 min   30 min

INGREDIENTS

4 servings

For the Stuffed Zucchini Boats:
4 medium zucchini, halved lengthwise
1 tbsp olive oil
1 small onion, finely chopped
2 cloves garlic, minced
1/2 cup cherry tomatoes, diced
1/2 cup cooked chickpeas, mashed slightly
1/2 tsp dried basil
1/2 tsp dried oregano
Salt and freshly ground black pepper, to taste

For the Cashew Parmesan:
1/2 cup raw cashews
2 tbsp nutritional yeast
1/4 tsp garlic powder
Salt, to taste

Allergens

CONTAINS NUTS

INSTRUCTIONS

Prepare the Zucchini Boats
- Preheat oven to 375°F (190°C).
- Hollow out zucchini halves and reserve the scooped-out zucchini flesh for the filling.
- Place the zucchini boats in a baking dish, lightly drizzling with olive oil and a pinch of salt and pepper. Bake for 10 minutes to soften slightly.

Prepare the Filling
- While the zucchini are baking, heat 1 tablespoon of olive oil in a skillet over medium heat. Add the onion and cook for 3-4 minutes until softened.
- Add the garlic and cook for another minute until fragrant.
- Stir in the cherry tomatoes, chickpeas, and reserved zucchini flesh, cooking for about 5 minutes until tender. Season with basil, oregano, salt, and pepper to taste.

Make the Cashew Parmesan
- In a food processor, combine the cashews, nutritional yeast, garlic powder, and a pinch of salt. Pulse until the mixture reaches a crumbly, Parmesan-like texture. Be careful not to over-process, as it can turn into cashew butter.

Stuff & bake the Zucchini Boats
- Remove the zucchini from the oven and fill them with vegetable-chickpea mixture, pressing down lightly to pack them full.
- Sprinkle a generous amount of cashew Parmesan on top of each stuffed zucchini and bake for 15-20 minutes until tender and golden.

Serve
- Garnish with fresh basil leaves if desired and serve warm.

CHEF'S TIPS

Extra Flavor: Add a sprinkle of red pepper flakes to the filling for a touch of heat, or a splash of balsamic vinegar for a hint of sweetness.

Variations: For a heartier version, add cooked quinoa or rice to the filling, or replace chickpeas with cannellini beans for a creamier texture.

CHAPTER

04

Contorni
(Side Dishes)

Overview

In Italian cuisine, **contorni** are essential vegetable-based side dishes that enhance meals with color and flavor. They feature seasonal produce and classic Mediterranean ingredients, such as olive oil and herbs. Examples include roasted eggplant, fresh salads, and sautéed zucchini. These dishes complement main courses or can be enjoyed alone, embodying the vibrant spirit of Italian cuisine and celebrating natural ingredients.

Discover additional contorni inspiration at *FreshPlantBased.com*!

Grilled Asparagus with Lemon Zest

Imagine vibrant green asparagus spears grilled to tender-crisp perfection, featuring smoky char marks that enhance their sweetness. This Grilled Asparagus with Lemon Zest combines earthy asparagus flavors with bright lemon notes, topped with fresh parsley for a refreshing side dish. With minimal ingredients, it's perfect for summer meals or as a light appetizer.

Wine Pairing: Verdicchio or a Pinot Gris

Difficulty

 5 min   10 min

INGREDIENTS

4 servings

1 lb fresh asparagus, trimmed
1 tbsp olive oil
Zest of 1 lemon
Salt and freshly ground black pepper, to taste
Fresh parsley, chopped, for garnish
Lemon wedges, for serving

Allergens

INSTRUCTIONS

Prepare the Asparagus
- Preheat a grill or grill pan over medium-high heat.
- In a large mixing bowl, toss the asparagus with olive oil, salt, and freshly ground black pepper until evenly coated.

Grill the Asparagus
- Place the asparagus on the grill in a single layer. Grill for 4-5 minutes, turning occasionally, until the asparagus is tender-crisp and has visible grill marks.

Add Lemon Zest
- Transfer the grilled asparagus to a serving plate. While still warm, sprinkle the lemon zest over the asparagus, allowing the warmth of the spears to release the citrusy aroma.

Serve
- Garnish with freshly chopped parsley and serve with lemon wedges for an extra squeeze of fresh lemon juice.

CHEF'S TIPS

Extra Flavor: Drizzle a little balsamic glaze over the asparagus just before serving to add a touch of sweetness that balances the lemon.

Variations: Add a sprinkle of vegan Parmesan or toasted pine nuts for added texture and flavor.

Garlic-Roasted Artichokes

Imagine tender, golden artichoke halves, crisped and caramelized in the oven, infused with roasted garlic and fresh herbs. These Garlic-Roasted Artichokes blend earthy and savory flavors, featuring smoky petals with a tangy lemon finish and a creamy heart. Perfect for sharing, this dish offers a delightful way to savor artichokes with a simple preparation.

Wine Pairing: Vermentino or a Chardonnay

Difficulty

10 min   40 min

INGREDIENTS

4 servings

4 large artichokes, trimmed and halved

3 tbsp olive oil

4 cloves garlic, sliced thinly

1 lemon, juiced, plus extra wedges for serving

1/2 tsp salt

Freshly ground black pepper, to taste

1 tsp fresh rosemary, finely chopped (or 1/2 tsp dried)

Fresh parsley, chopped, for garnish

Allergens

INSTRUCTIONS

Prepare the Artichokes

- Preheat your oven to 400°F (200°C).
- Start by trimming the artichokes. Remove the tough outer leaves and cut off the top third of each artichoke. Slice them in half lengthwise and use a spoon to scoop out the fuzzy choke from the center.
- Place the artichoke halves in a bowl of water with a few drops of lemon juice to prevent browning while you prepare the other ingredients.

Season the Artichokes

- Drain the artichokes and pat them dry. Place them cut-side up in a baking dish.
- Drizzle the olive oil over the artichokes, coating each one generously. Tuck the garlic slices in between the petals and around the artichokes.
- Squeeze the lemon juice over the artichokes and sprinkle with salt, black pepper, and chopped rosemary. Toss everything gently to ensure the flavors are well distributed.

Roast the Artichokes

- Cover the baking dish with foil and roast the artichokes in the preheated oven for 30 minutes.
- After 30 minutes, remove the foil and continue roasting for another 10-15 minutes, or until the artichokes are golden and tender, with slightly crispy edges.

Serve

- Transfer the garlic-roasted artichokes to a serving platter. Garnish with freshly chopped parsley and serve with extra lemon wedges for added brightness.

CHEF'S TIPS

Extra Flavor: For a burst of umami, add a drizzle of balsamic glaze or a sprinkle of vegan Parmesan over the artichokes just before serving.

Variations: Try adding a pinch of crushed red pepper flakes for a subtle kick, or replace rosemary with fresh thyme for a different herbaceous note.

Sautéed Broccolini with Chili Flakes and Garlic

Sautéed Broccolini with Chili Flakes and Garlic is a vibrant and flavorful side dish. Quick to prepare, it features crisp-tender broccolini coated in golden garlic and a hint of red chili flakes for heat. The slightly bitter broccolini balances the sweetness of garlic and the zing of chili, creating a delightful contrast of flavors and textures, making it a perfect accompaniment to any main course.

Wine Pairing: Pinot Grigio or a Sauvignon Blanc

Difficulty

5 min   10 min

INGREDIENTS

4 servings

1 lb broccolini, ends trimmed
2 tbsp olive oil
3 cloves garlic, thinly sliced
1/2 tsp red chili flakes (adjust to taste)
Salt and freshly ground black pepper, to taste
1 lemon, zest and juice
Fresh parsley, chopped, for garnish

Allergens

INSTRUCTIONS

Blanch the Broccolini
- Boil broccolini in salted water for 2-3 minutes, until it turns a vibrant green but is still crisp then transfer to ice water. Drain again and set aside.

Sauté the Garlic
- In a skillet, heat the olive oil over medium heat. Add the garlic and sauté for 1-2 minutes until it turns golden.

Add the Broccolini and Chili Flakes
- Add the blanched broccolini to the skillet, tossing to coat it in the garlic-infused oil. Sprinkle in the red chili flakes and season with salt and black pepper.
- Sauté the broccolini for about 3-5 minutes, until it is tender-crisp and warmed through, with a slight char starting to form.

Finish with Lemon Zest and Juice
- Remove the skillet from the heat. Zest the lemon over the broccolini, then squeeze the lemon juice on top, tossing everything gently to coat.

Serve
- Transfer the broccolini to a serving platter, garnish with fresh parsley, and serve warm.

CHEF'S TIPS

Extra Flavor: For an added depth, drizzle a small amount of balsamic vinegar over the broccolini just before serving, adding a touch of sweetness that complements the chili and garlic.

Variations: Substitute broccolini with tenderstem broccoli or regular broccoli florets for a similar texture and taste. If you prefer a smoky flavor, add a sprinkle of smoked paprika with the chili flakes.

Rosemary and Olive Oil Roasted Potatoes

Imagine golden, crispy potatoes with a warm, herbaceous aroma as they roast. Rosemary and Olive Oil Roasted Potatoes offer a satisfying blend of crispy edges and fluffy interiors, infused with rosemary and garlic. This simple yet luxurious side complements any main course, adding rustic charm to family dinners or festive gatherings, and is easy to prepare, making it a kitchen favorite.

Wine Pairing: Chianti or a Zinfandel

Difficulty

10 min   35 min

INGREDIENTS

4 servings

2 lbs Yukon Gold or baby
potatoes, washed and quartered
3 tbsp extra virgin olive oil
2 tbsp fresh rosemary, finely
chopped (or 1 tbsp dried
rosemary)
3 cloves garlic, minced
Salt and freshly ground black
pepper, to taste
Fresh parsley, chopped, for
garnish

Allergens

INSTRUCTIONS

Preheat the Oven
- Preheat your oven to 425°F (220°C). Line a baking sheet with parchment paper or lightly grease it with olive oil to prevent sticking.

Season the Potatoes
- In a large mixing bowl, combine the quartered potatoes with olive oil, chopped rosemary, minced garlic, salt, and freshly ground black pepper. Toss until the potatoes are evenly coated.

Arrange on the Baking Sheet
- Spread the seasoned potatoes in a single layer on the prepared baking sheet, ensuring they have some space between them for even roasting.

Roast the Potatoes
- Roast in the preheated oven for 30-35 minutes, or until the potatoes are golden and crispy on the outside and tender on the inside. Flip the potatoes halfway through cooking to promote even browning.

Serve
- Remove the potatoes from the oven and transfer them to a serving dish. Garnish with freshly chopped parsley for a pop of color and a fresh finish.

CHEF'S TIPS

Extra Flavor: For a hint of tanginess, squeeze fresh lemon juice over the potatoes just before serving, or sprinkle with a touch of lemon zest for added brightness.

Variations: Swap rosemary with thyme or add a sprinkle of smoked paprika for a different flavor profile. You can also add a handful of halved cherry tomatoes to the potatoes during the last 10 minutes of roasting for a burst of color and flavor.

Marinated Grilled Vegetables

Imagine a plate of vibrant, charred vegetables marinated in rosemary, balsamic, and garlic. These Marinated Grilled Vegetables highlight seasonal produce, enhancing the natural sweetness of bell peppers, zucchini, eggplant, and mushrooms. Perfect for summer gatherings or as a side dish, they are easy to prepare and offer a delightful taste of rustic Italian flavors.

Wine Pairing: Vermentino or a Sauvignon Blanc

Difficulty

15 min   10 min

INGREDIENTS

4 servings

1 red bell pepper, seeded and cut into large strips

1 yellow bell pepper, seeded and cut into large strips

1 zucchini, sliced lengthwise into 1/4-inch strips

1 eggplant, sliced lengthwise into 1/4-inch strips

8 oz cremini mushrooms, stems removed

1/4 cup olive oil

3 tbsp balsamic vinegar

3 cloves garlic, minced

2 tsp fresh rosemary, chopped (or 1 tsp dried rosemary)

Salt and freshly ground black pepper, to taste

Fresh basil leaves, torn, for garnish (optional)

Allergens

INSTRUCTIONS

Prepare the Marinade
- In a mixing bowl, whisk together the olive oil, balsamic vinegar, garlic, rosemary, salt, and pepper.

Marinate the Vegetables
- Add the bell peppers, zucchini, eggplant, and mushrooms to the bowl with the marinade. Toss well to coat all the vegetables evenly.
- Cover and let marinate for at least 30 minutes.

Preheat the Grill
- Preheat a grill or grill pan over medium-high heat. Brush the grates lightly with olive oil to prevent sticking.

Grill the Vegetables
- Grill the vegetables in a single layer for about 3-5 minutes per side, or until they are tender and have visible char marks.
- The bell peppers and mushrooms may take a bit longer than the zucchini and eggplant so adjust timing as needed.

Serve
- Arrange on a serving platter and garnish with torn basil leaves for a fresh, aromatic finish, if desired.

CHEF'S TIPS

Extra Flavor: Add a sprinkle of crushed red pepper flakes to the marinade for a hint of heat, or a dash of smoked paprika for a smoky depth.

Variations: You can add other seasonal vegetables like asparagus, cherry tomatoes, or red onions for added color and flavor. Try topping the finished dish with a drizzle of lemon juice or vegan Parmesan for extra zest.

Vegan Caesar Salad with Crispy Chickpeas

This Vegan Caesar Salad is a fresh take on a classic, featuring crisp romaine, crunchy roasted chickpeas, creamy vegan dressing, and vegan Parmesan. The chickpeas provide protein and crunch, while the tangy dressing delivers bold flavors without dairy. It's ideal as a light main dish or a flavorful appetizer to impress guests.

Wine Pairing: Pinot Grigio or a Sauvignon Blanc

Difficulty

15 min

20 min

INGREDIENTS

4 servings

For the Salad:
1 large head of romaine lettuce, chopped
1/4 cup vegan Parmesan cheese, grated (optional)

For the Crispy Chickpeas:
1 can (15 oz) chickpeas, drained, rinsed, and patted dry
1 tbsp olive oil
1/2 tsp smoked paprika
1/2 tsp garlic powder
Salt and freshly ground black pepper, to taste

For the Vegan Caesar Dressing:
1/4 cup vegan mayonnaise
1 tbsp lemon juice
1 tsp Dijon mustard
1 tsp capers, finely chopped
1 clove garlic, minced
1 tsp vegan Worcestershire sauce (optional)
Salt and black pepper, to taste
2 tbsp water (to thin, if necessary)

Allergens

CONTAINS NUTS

INSTRUCTIONS

Prepare the Crispy Chickpeas
- Preheat your oven to 400°F (200°C) and line a baking sheet with parchment paper.
- In a mixing bowl, toss the chickpeas with olive oil, smoked paprika, garlic powder, salt, and black pepper. Spread them in a single layer on the baking sheet.
- Roast for 20 minutes, shaking the pan halfway through, until the chickpeas are crispy and golden brown. Remove from the oven and set aside to cool slightly.

Make the Vegan Caesar Dressing
- In a small bowl, whisk together the vegan mayonnaise, lemon juice, Dijon mustard, capers, minced garlic, and vegan Worcestershire sauce, if using.
- Season with salt and black pepper, then add water, one tablespoon at a time, until the dressing reaches your desired consistency. Set aside.

Assemble the Salad
- In a large salad bowl, add the chopped romaine lettuce. Drizzle with the Caesar dressing and toss to coat the leaves evenly.
- Sprinkle the crispy chickpeas on top, followed by a generous amount of grated vegan Parmesan.

Serve
- Divide the salad among four plates, garnishing with extra chickpeas or vegan Parmesan if desired. Serve immediately to enjoy the crisp textures.

CHEF'S TIPS

Extra Flavor: Add a pinch of red pepper flakes to the dressing for a hint of heat or a sprinkle of lemon zest to brighten the flavors.

Variations: For added texture, try mixing in sliced avocado or cherry tomatoes. You can also replace the chickpeas with roasted almonds or sunflower seeds for a different crunch.

Balsamic—Glazed Carrots with Thyme

These Balsamic-Glazed Carrots with Thyme are visually appealing and flavorful, featuring vibrant orange carrots glazed with reduced balsamic vinegar and fresh thyme. The dish combines natural sweetness with tanginess and earthy notes, making it an elegant side for special occasions. Each bite offers a delightful balance of flavors and textures, ensuring the carrots shine on the dining table.

Wine Pairing: Chianti or a Pinot Noir

Difficulty

10 min   20 min

INGREDIENTS

4 servings

1 lb carrots, peeled and cut into sticks or rounds
1 tbsp olive oil
2 tbsp balsamic vinegar
1 tbsp maple syrup (or agave syrup)
1 tsp fresh thyme leaves (or 1/2 tsp dried thyme)
Salt and freshly ground black pepper, to taste
Fresh parsley, chopped, for garnish (optional)

Allergens

INSTRUCTIONS

Prepare the Carrots
- In a large skillet over medium heat, add the olive oil. Once heated, add the carrots and sauté for 5-7 minutes, stirring occasionally, until they start to soften and develop a light golden color.

Add the Glaze Ingredients
- In a small bowl, whisk together the balsamic vinegar and maple syrup until well combined. Pour this mixture over the carrots, stirring to coat them evenly.

Cook with Thyme
- Add the fresh thyme leaves to the skillet and season with a pinch of salt and black pepper. Continue cooking for an additional 10 minutes, stirring occasionally, until the balsamic mixture thickens and glazes the carrots, making sure they are tender but still hold their shape.

Serve
- Transfer the glazed carrots to a serving platter, garnishing with freshly chopped parsley for a burst of color if desired. Serve warm.

CHEF'S TIPS

Extra Flavor: Add a sprinkle of crushed red pepper flakes for a hint of spice or a touch of lemon zest for added brightness.

Variations: You can substitute thyme with rosemary for a woodier, more aromatic flavor or try adding a handful of toasted pine nuts on top for extra crunch.

Sautéed Spinach with Pine Nuts and Raisins

This Sautéed Spinach with Pine Nuts and Raisins showcases Italian simplicity with tender spinach wilted in olive oil and garlic, complemented by sweet golden raisins and crunchy pine nuts. The dish harmonizes earthy greens, nutty aroma, and slight sweetness, making it a vibrant and elegant side suitable for any occasion.

Wine Pairing: Verdicchio or a Chardonnay

Difficulty

5 min   10 min

INGREDIENTS

4 servings

2 tbsp olive oil
2 cloves garlic, thinly sliced
10 oz fresh spinach, washed and dried
1/4 cup pine nuts
1/4 cup golden raisins
Salt and freshly ground black pepper, to taste
Fresh lemon wedges, for serving

Allergens

CONTAINS
NUTS

INSTRUCTIONS

Toast the Pine Nuts

- In a large skillet over medium heat, add the pine nuts and toast them for 2-3 minutes, stirring frequently, until they are golden brown and aromatic. Be careful not to let them burn. Transfer the toasted pine nuts to a small bowl and set aside.

Sauté the Garlic

- In the same skillet, heat the olive oil over medium heat. Add the sliced garlic and sauté for about 1 minute, or until it becomes fragrant and golden. Avoid browning the garlic too much, as it can become bitter.

Add Spinach, Raisins, and Seasoning

- Add the fresh spinach and golden raisins to the skillet with the garlic. Season with a pinch of salt and black pepper. Cook, stirring occasionally, for 3-5 minutes, or until the spinach is wilted but still vibrant green, and the raisins have softened slightly.

Combine with Pine Nuts

- Return the toasted pine nuts to the skillet, stirring to combine them with the spinach and raisins. Cook for another minute to warm everything through.

Serve

- Transfer the sautéed spinach mixture to a serving dish. Serve with fresh lemon wedges for an optional squeeze of brightness.

CHEF'S TIPS

Extra Flavor: Add a sprinkle of crushed red pepper flakes for a hint of spice or a touch of lemon zest for added brightness.

Variations: You can substitute thyme with rosemary for a woodier, more aromatic flavor or try adding a handful of toasted pine nuts on top for extra crunch.

Vegan Panzanella (Italian Bread Salad)

This Sautéed Spinach with Pine Nuts and Raisins showcases Italian simplicity with tender spinach wilted in olive oil and garlic, complemented by sweet golden raisins and crunchy pine nuts. The dish harmonizes earthy greens, nutty aroma, and slight sweetness, making it a vibrant and elegant side suitable for any occasion.

Wine Pairing: Vermentino or a Sauvignon Blanc

Difficulty

15 min   10 min

INGREDIENTS

4 servings

4 cups day-old crusty bread, cut into 1-inch cubes
1 cup cherry tomatoes, halved
1 medium cucumber, diced
1/2 red onion, thinly sliced
1/4 cup fresh basil leaves, torn
1/4 cup extra virgin olive oil
2 tbsp red wine vinegar
Salt and freshly ground black pepper, to taste

Allergens

CONTAINS NUTS

INSTRUCTIONS

Toast the Bread
- Preheat your oven to 375°F (190°C). Spread the bread cubes on a baking sheet and toast in the oven for 8-10 minutes, or until golden and crisp. Allow the bread to cool slightly.

Prepare the Vegetables
- In a large mixing bowl, combine the halved cherry tomatoes, diced cucumber, and thinly sliced red onion. Add the torn basil leaves and toss gently to combine.

Make the Dressing
- In a small bowl, whisk together the extra virgin olive oil, red wine vinegar, salt, and black pepper until emulsified.

Combine and Toss
- Add the toasted bread cubes to the bowl with the vegetables. Pour the dressing over the salad and toss everything together until the bread is well coated and begins to absorb the juices.

Rest and Serve
- Allow the Panzanella to sit for about 10-15 minutes to let the flavors meld and for the bread to soak up the dressing. Serve at room temperature.

CHEF'S TIPS

Extra Flavor: For an additional burst of flavor, add capers or sliced Kalamata olives to the salad, which bring a briny contrast to the sweetness of the tomatoes.

Variations: Substitute cherry tomatoes with heirloom tomatoes for more color, or add a handful of arugula for a peppery kick. You can also drizzle a bit of balsamic glaze on top for a touch of sweetness.

Roasted Cauliflower with Lemon and Capers

Imagine golden cauliflower florets, perfectly roasted until caramelized and crisp with a tender interior. This Roasted Cauliflower with Lemon and Capers features nutty flavors, bright lemon acidity, and briny capers, creating a light yet elegant side dish. Easy to prepare and full of vibrant flavors, it's ideal for weeknight meals or festive dinners.

Wine Pairing: Pinot Grigio or a Chardonnay

Difficulty

10 min   30 min

INGREDIENTS

4 servings

1 large head of cauliflower, cut into bite-sized florets
3 tbsp olive oil
Salt and freshly ground black pepper, to taste
Zest of 1 lemon
2 tbsp capers, drained
2 tbsp fresh parsley, chopped, for garnish
Lemon wedges, for serving

Allergens

INSTRUCTIONS

Preheat the Oven
- Preheat your oven to 425°F (220°C). Line a large baking sheet with parchment paper or lightly grease it with olive oil to prevent sticking.

Season the Cauliflower
- In a large bowl, toss the cauliflower florets with olive oil, salt, and black pepper, ensuring they are evenly coated. Spread the florets in a single layer on the prepared baking sheet.

Roast the Cauliflower
- Roast the cauliflower in the preheated oven for 25-30 minutes, or until the florets are tender and their edges are golden and crispy. Toss them halfway through to ensure even browning.

Add Lemon Zest and Capers
- Once the cauliflower is done, remove it from the oven and transfer it to a large serving bowl. Add the lemon zest and capers, tossing gently to combine.

Serve
- Garnish with freshly chopped parsley and serve warm with lemon wedges on the side for an extra squeeze of brightness.

CHEF'S TIPS

Extra Flavor: For an added layer of richness, drizzle a bit of tahini or a touch of vegan Parmesan over the cauliflower before serving.

Variations: Add a pinch of red pepper flakes for a bit of heat or substitute capers with sliced olives for a different briny flavor.

CHAPTER
05
Dolci
(Desserts)

Overview

In Italian cuisine, **dolci** (desserts) embody the art of turning simple ingredients into elegant creations. In a plant-based context, these desserts retain their authenticity and flavor using alternatives like cashew cream, aquafaba, and coconut milk. Classics such as tiramisu are made with plant-based mascarpone, while gelatos shine with almond or oat milk bases. From crostata to panna cotta, plant-based dolci bring the joy of Italian dessert-making to life, offering indulgent yet wholesome sweet moments.

Get more delicious dolci recipes at *FreshPlantBased.com*!

Vegan Tiramisu with Coconut Cream

This Vegan Tiramisu with Coconut Cream is a rich, plant-based version of the classic Italian dessert. It features layers of coffee-soaked ladyfingers and creamy coconut filling with vanilla, topped with cocoa powder. Each bite offers a delightful blend of creamy textures and strong espresso flavors, making it a captivating dessert for any occasion.

Wine Pairing: Vin Santo or a Late Harvest Riesling

Difficulty

20 min   10 min

INGREDIENTS

4 servings

For the Coconut Cream Filling:
1 can (14 oz) full-fat coconut milk, chilled overnight
1 cup raw cashews, soaked for 4 hours or overnight, then drained
1/4 cup powdered sugar or maple syrup
1 tsp vanilla extract

For the Coffee Soak:
1 cup strong brewed espresso or coffee, cooled
2 tbsp coffee liqueur (optional, or replace with more coffee)
2 tbsp maple syrup

For Assembly:
1 package vegan ladyfingers or sponge cake (if unavailable, use vegan graham crackers or biscotti)
2 tbsp cocoa powder, for dusting
Fresh mint leaves, for garnish (optional)

Allergens

CONTAINS GLUTEN   CONTAINS NUTS

INSTRUCTIONS

Prepare the Coconut Cream Filling
- Open the chilled can of coconut milk and scoop out the solid coconut cream into a mixing bowl, discarding the liquid or saving it for another use.
- In a high-speed blender or food processor, combine the coconut cream, soaked cashews, powdered sugar or maple syrup, and vanilla extract. Blend until smooth and creamy, scraping down the sides as needed. Set aside.

Make the Coffee Soak
- In a shallow bowl, mix the brewed espresso, coffee liqueur (if using), and maple syrup. Stir well and set aside to cool completely.

Assemble the Tiramisu
- Dip each ladyfinger briefly into the coffee soak, making sure it's soaked but not soggy, and lay them in a single layer in the bottom of a serving dish or individual dessert cups.
- Spread a layer of the coconut cream mixture over the soaked ladyfingers, smoothing it out with a spatula.
- Repeat with another layer of soaked ladyfingers, followed by another layer of coconut cream. Continue layering until you've used all the ingredients, finishing with a layer of coconut cream on top.

Chill and Dust with Cocoa
- Cover the tiramisu and refrigerate for at least 4 hours, or preferably overnight, to allow the flavors to meld and the dessert to firm up.
- Just before serving, dust the top generously with cocoa powder and garnish with fresh mint leaves if desired.

CHEF'S TIPS

Extra Flavor: Add a pinch of cinnamon to the coffee soak for a subtle, warming spice that complements the coconut cream.

Variations: For a twist, add a layer of finely chopped dark chocolate or chocolate shavings between layers for a richer flavor.

Almond Biscotti Dipped in Dark Chocolate

Almond Biscotti Dipped in Dark Chocolate are a delightful treat, perfect with coffee or dessert wine. They are golden-brown, crunchy, and filled with toasted almonds, offering a satisfying snap and rich flavor. Dipped in velvety dark chocolate, these elegant cookies are ideal for special occasions or simple moments of enjoyment.

Wine Pairing: Vin Santo or a Zinfandel

Difficulty

20 min   45 min

INGREDIENTS

4 servings

1 cup almond flour
1 cup all-purpose flour (use gluten-free flour for a gluten-free option)
1 tsp baking powder
1/2 cup sugar
1/4 cup almond milk
1/4 cup coconut oil, melted
1 tsp vanilla extract
1/2 tsp almond extract
1/2 cup whole almonds, roughly chopped
4 oz dark chocolate, melted, for dipping

Allergens

CONTAINS   CONTAINS
GLUTEN   NUTS

INSTRUCTIONS

Preheat the Oven
- Preheat your oven to 350°F (175°C). Line a baking sheet with parchment paper.

Mix the Dry and Wet Ingredients
- In a bowl, mix almond flour, all-purpose flour, baking powder, and sugar. Stir well to mix the ingredients evenly.
- In a separate bowl, whisk together the almond milk, melted coconut oil, vanilla extract, and almond extract. Mix wet ingredients into dry to form a dough.

Incorporate the Almonds
- Fold in the chopped almonds, evenly distributed.

Shape & Bake the Biscotti
- Shape the dough into 10x3-inch log wide. Flatten the top slightly for even baking.
- Bake for 25-30 minutes until firm and golden. Remove from the oven and allow it to cool for about 10 minutes.

Slice and Second Bake
- Once cool enough slice the log into 1/2-inch thick biscotti pieces. Place the slices cut-side down and bake for 10-15 minutes, flipping them halfway, until crisp and golden. Remove from the oven and let cool.

Dip in Dark Chocolate
- Once the biscotti have cooled, dip one end of each biscotto into the melted dark chocolate and let set on parchment.

Serve
- Enjoy with coffee, tea, or dessert wine.

CHEF'S TIPS

Extra Flavor: Add a pinch of cinnamon or a few drops of orange zest to the dough for a warm, spiced flavor that complements the dark chocolate.

Variations: Try using pistachios or hazelnuts instead of almonds for a unique twist. You can also drizzle the biscotti with white chocolate for an elegant finish.

Vegan Panna Cotta with Berry Compote

This Vegan Panna Cotta with Berry Compote is a sophisticated Italian dessert that is silky, creamy, and infused with vanilla and coconut. The rich yet light texture is complemented by a vibrant berry compote, balancing creamy sweetness with tart berries. It's a perfect finish for any meal, whether for celebration or indulgence.

Wine Pairing: Moscato d'Asti or a Late Harvest Riesling

Difficulty

10 min   10 min

INGREDIENTS

4 servings

For the Panna Cotta:
1 can (14 oz) full-fat coconut milk
1 cup almond milk (or other plant milk)
1/4 cup maple syrup (or agave syrup)
1 tsp vanilla extract
1/2 tsp agar agar powder (or 1 tsp agar agar flakes)

For the Berry Compote:
1 cup mixed berries (strawberries, blueberries, raspberries)
2 tbsp maple syrup (or sugar)
1 tbsp lemon juice
Zest of 1/2 lemon

Allergens

CONTAINS NUTS

INSTRUCTIONS

Prepare the Panna Cotta Mixture
- In a saucepan, whisk the coconut milk, almond milk, maple syrup, and vanilla extract.
- Sprinkle the agar agar powder evenly over the liquid and whisk to incorporate. Let the mixture sit for a minute or two to allow the agar to hydrate.

Cook the Panna Cotta
- Place the saucepan over medium heat and bring the mixture to a simmer, whisking frequently. Once it starts to simmer, continue cooking for 2-3 minutes, ensuring the agar agar fully dissolves. Avoid boiling to keep the panna cotta smooth.

Pour and Set
- Pour the warm mixture into four small serving glasses or molds. Allow them to cool to room temperature, then cover and refrigerate for at least 2 hours or until the panna cotta is firm and set.

Make the Berry Compote
- In a small saucepan, combine the berries, maple syrup, lemon juice, and lemon zest. Cook over medium heat for 5-7 minutes, stirring occasionally, until the berries break down and the mixture thickens slightly. Remove from heat and let the compote cool to room temperature.

Serve
- Once the panna cotta has set, spoon a generous amount of berry compote over each serving. Garnish with a few fresh berries or a sprig of mint if desired.

CHEF'S TIPS

Extra Flavor: Add a pinch of cinnamon or a dash of almond extract to the panna cotta mixture for a warm, nutty note.

Variations: Try using other fruits for the compote, like cherries or peaches, for a seasonal twist, or drizzle with a balsamic reduction for a sophisticated finish.

Orange and Olive Oil Cake

This Orange and Olive Oil Cake combines fresh orange zest and high-quality olive oil for a flavorful dessert. It features a soft, moist texture with citrus notes and subtle fruitiness from the olive oil. Finished with powdered sugar or orange glaze, it offers a light, airy, and sophisticated Italian flair, perfect for any occasion.

Wine Pairing: Moscato d'Asti or a Sparkling Brut

Difficulty

15 min   40 min

INGREDIENTS

4 *servings*

1/2 cups all-purpose flour
3/4 cup granulated sugar
1/2 cup extra virgin olive oil
Zest of 2 large oranges
1/2 cup freshly squeezed orange juice
1/4 cup almond milk (or other plant-based milk)
1 tsp vanilla extract
1 1/2 tsp baking powder
1/2 tsp baking soda
1/4 tsp salt
Powdered sugar, for dusting (optional)

Allergens

CONTAINS GLUTEN

INSTRUCTIONS

Preheat the Oven
- Preheat your oven to 350°F (175°C). Grease an 8-inch round cake pan and line the bottom with parchment paper for easy removal.

Mix the Wet Ingredients
- In a large mixing bowl, whisk together the olive oil, sugar, orange zest, orange juice, almond milk, and vanilla extract until smooth and well combined.

Combine the Dry Ingredients
- In a separate bowl, sift together the all-purpose flour, baking powder, baking soda, and salt. Stir to ensure the dry ingredients are evenly distributed.

Create the Batter
- Gradually add the dry ingredients to the wet ingredients, folding gently until just combined. Be careful not to overmix, as this can make the cake dense.

Bake the Cake
- Pour the batter into the prepared cake pan and smooth the top with a spatula. Bake in the preheated oven for 35-40 minutes, or until a toothpick inserted in the center comes out clean and the top is golden brown.

Cool and Serve
- Allow the cake to cool in the pan for 10 minutes before transferring it to a wire rack to cool completely. Once cooled, dust with powdered sugar or drizzle with a simple orange glaze if desired.

CHEF'S TIPS

Extra Flavor: Add a pinch of cinnamon or cardamom to the batter for a warm, spiced note that complements the orange and olive oil.

Variations: Drizzle the cake with a glaze made from 1/2 cup powdered sugar mixed with 1-2 tablespoons of fresh orange juice for a zesty finish. You can also sprinkle toasted almonds on top for added texture.

Cannoli with Cashew Cream

Cannoli are a classic Italian dessert, and this vegan version offers a delightful twist. It features crisp shells filled with a creamy cashew filling flavored with vanilla and citrus. Each bite combines a satisfying crunch with smooth cream, creating a perfect texture balance. Topped with powdered sugar and optional dark chocolate chips or pistachios, these Cannoli with Cashew Cream are both enjoyable to eat and visually appealing.

Wine Pairing: Moscato d'Asti or a Sparkling Rosé

Difficulty

20 min   10 min

INGREDIENTS

4 servings

For the Cashew Cream Filling:
1 cup raw cashews, soaked overnight or for at least 4 hours, then drained
1/4 cup almond or coconut milk
2 tbsp maple syrup or agave syrup
1 tsp vanilla extract
Zest of 1/2 orange
1/4 tsp salt

For the Cannoli Shells (use store-bought vegan shells or make homemade):
8 small vegan cannoli shells (can substitute gluten-free if needed)

For Garnish:
2 tbsp powdered sugar, for dusting
2 tbsp mini dark chocolate chips or finely chopped dark chocolate (optional)
2 tbsp finely chopped pistachios (optional)

Allergens

CONTAINS GLUTEN   CONTAINS NUTS

INSTRUCTIONS

Prepare the Cashew Cream
- In a high-speed blender or food processor, combine the soaked and drained cashews, almond milk, maple syrup, vanilla extract, orange zest, and salt.
- Blend until the mixture is smooth and creamy, scraping down the sides as needed. The filling should be thick but spreadable. If it's too thick, add a little more almond milk, one teaspoon at a time, until you reach the desired consistency.

Chill the Filling
- Transfer the cashew cream to a bowl, cover, and refrigerate for at least 30 minutes. This will help the cream firm up and enhance the flavors.

Fill the Cannoli Shells
- Once the filling is chilled, spoon it into a piping bag fitted with a round tip (or use a plastic zip-top bag and snip off one corner). Carefully pipe the cashew cream into each end of the cannoli shells, filling them completely.

Garnish
- For an extra touch, dip the ends of the filled cannoli in mini dark chocolate chips or chopped pistachios. Dust with powdered sugar just before serving for a classic finish.

Serve
- Serve the cannoli fresh to enjoy the contrast of the crispy shells with the creamy filling.

CHEF'S TIPS

Extra Flavor: For a more traditional flavor, add a touch of almond extract to the filling, or fold in finely chopped candied orange peel for added texture.

Variations: Try adding a pinch of cinnamon or a dash of cocoa powder to the cashew cream for a warm, spiced variation. You could also experiment with a chocolate-dipped shell for an extra layer of indulgence.

Chocolate Hazelnut Tart

This Chocolate Hazelnut Tart is an indulgent Italian dessert featuring a crispy, buttery crust and a rich filling of dark chocolate and roasted hazelnuts. The combination of velvety chocolate and nutty hazelnuts creates a delightful balance of flavors. Topped with sea salt or cocoa powder, it's ideal for special occasions or to add decadence to any meal.

Wine Pairing: Barolo Chinato or a Zinfandel

Difficulty

20 min   15 min

INGREDIENTS

4 servings

For the Crust:
1 cup almond flour
1/2 cup all-purpose flour (or gluten-free flour for a gluten-free option)
2 tbsp coconut sugar
1/4 cup coconut oil, melted
Pinch of salt

For the Chocolate Hazelnut Filling:
1 cup full-fat coconut milk
6 oz dark chocolate, chopped
1/4 cup hazelnut butter (or almond butter as a substitute)
1/4 cup maple syrup
1 tsp vanilla extract
Pinch of sea salt

For Garnish:
1/4 cup roasted hazelnuts, chopped
Cocoa powder or sea salt, for sprinkling

Allergens

CONTAINS GLUTEN   CONTAINS NUTS

INSTRUCTIONS

Prepare the Crust
- Preheat the oven to 350°F (175°C). Grease a 9-inch tart pan with a removable bottom.
- In a bowl mix the almond flour, all-purpose flour, coconut sugar, melted coconut oil, and salt until the mixture resembles wet sand.
- Press into a greased tart pan, smoothing evenly.

Bake the Crust
- Bake the crust for 10-12 minutes until golden.
- Remove from the oven and allow it to cool completely.

Make the Chocolate Hazelnut Filling
- In a saucepan, heat the coconut milk over medium heat until simmering. Remove from heat, stir in dark chocolate until smooth.
- Mix well the hazelnut butter, maple syrup, vanilla extract, and a pinch of salt until creamy and fully combined.

Fill the Tart
- Pour filling into cooled crust, smooth the top for a polished look, and sprinkle with roasted hazelnuts.

Chill the Tart
- Refrigerate the tart for at least 1 hour until set.

Serve
- Just before serving, dust the tart lightly with cocoa powder or sprinkle with a small amount of sea salt for an added layer of flavor.

CHEF'S TIPS

Extra Flavor: Add a splash of hazelnut liqueur to the filling for a deeper hazelnut flavor or a pinch of espresso powder to enhance the chocolate notes.

Variations: For a more textured filling, fold in a few chopped hazelnuts into the chocolate mixture before pouring it into the crust. You can also top the tart with fresh.

Strawberry Basil Granita

This Strawberry Basil Granita is a refreshing dessert that combines sweet strawberries with aromatic basil. It offers a burst of flavor in each icy spoonful, making it ideal for summer or as a light addition to meals. Visually stunning and easy to prepare, it captures the essence of Italian summer in every bite.

Wine Pairing: Prosecco or a Sparkling Rosé

Difficulty

10 min

INGREDIENTS

4 servings

1 lb fresh strawberries, hulled
1/4 cup fresh basil leaves
1/2 cup water
1/4 cup maple syrup (or sugar, to taste)
1 tbsp fresh lemon juice

Allergens

INSTRUCTIONS

Blend the Ingredients
- In a blender or food processor, combine the strawberries, basil leaves, water, maple syrup, and lemon juice. Blend until smooth, ensuring that the basil is fully incorporated for a consistent flavor.

Strain (Optional)
- For a smoother texture, pour the blended mixture through a fine-mesh sieve into a bowl to remove any seeds and basil bits. This step is optional but recommended for a refined finish.

Freeze the Mixture
- Pour the strained mixture into a shallow baking dish, spreading it out evenly. Place the dish in the freezer.
- Scrape to Create the Granita Texture
- After about 1 hour, use a fork to scrape the edges of the granita, pulling the frozen bits toward the center. Return to the freezer and repeat this scraping process every 30-45 minutes until the entire mixture is frozen and has a fluffy, icy texture. This should take 2-3 hours in total.

Serve
- Spoon the granita into chilled glasses or bowls, garnish with a small basil leaf or a fresh strawberry slice if desired, and serve immediately.

CHEF'S TIPS

Extra Flavor: For a slightly spicier note, add a pinch of freshly ground black pepper to the mixture before freezing. Black pepper complements strawberries beautifully, adding depth to the flavor.

Variations: Experiment with different herbs such as mint or thyme instead of basil for a new twist. You can also mix in a splash of balsamic vinegar to enhance the strawberry flavor.

Affogato with Vegan Vanilla Gelato

The Affogato is a luxurious Italian dessert featuring creamy vanilla gelato topped with hot espresso. This vegan version retains classic flavors while using plant-based ingredients, blending the intense coffee with smooth vegan gelato. The combination of hot and cold, bitter and sweet creates a delightful contrast, making it an ideal after-dinner treat that offers sweetness and a caffeine boost.

Wine Pairing: Amaro (for a classic Italian touch or a Espresso Martini)

Difficulty

5 min   5 min

INGREDIENTS

4 servings

4 scoops vegan vanilla gelato (coconut, almond, or cashew-based works well)
4 shots of hot espresso (about 1 oz each)
Dark chocolate shavings or cocoa powder, for garnish (optional)

Allergens

INSTRUCTIONS

Prepare the Espresso

- Brew four shots of espresso using an espresso machine, moka pot, or French press. The espresso should be hot and freshly made, as it will be poured immediately over the gelato.

Scoop the Gelato

- Place one scoop of vegan vanilla gelato into each serving cup or glass. For an elegant presentation, use chilled glass bowls or espresso cups.

Pour the Espresso Over the Gelato

- Pour one shot of hot espresso over each scoop of gelato. Serve immediately to enjoy the melting effect, which creates a beautiful mix of creamy and frothy textures.

Garnish

- If desired, garnish with a sprinkle of dark chocolate shavings or a light dusting of cocoa powder for added depth and a touch of elegance.

CHEF'S TIPS

Extra Flavor: Add a drop of almond extract or a splash of amaretto liqueur to the espresso before pouring for a subtle nutty twist.

Variations: Try experimenting with different flavors of vegan gelato, such as chocolate, hazelnut, or coconut, to create new and unique affogato combinations. You could also add a sprinkle of cinnamon or a pinch of sea salt for an extra layer of flavor.

Lemon Almond Ricotta Cake

This Lemon Almond Ricotta Cake is a refreshing dessert featuring fresh lemon zest and creamy almond ricotta. Each slice is moist, fluffy, and flavorful, with a subtle nuttiness from the almond. Topped with a lemon glaze or powdered sugar, it is a beautiful and delicious choice for spring gatherings or elegant meals.

Wine Pairing: Moscato d'Asti or a Sparkling Chardonnay

Difficulty

15 min   40 min

INGREDIENTS

4 servings

For the Cake:
1 1/4 cups almond flour
1 cup all-purpose flour (or gluten-free flour if needed)
1 cup vegan almond ricotta (store-bought or homemade)
3/4 cup granulated sugar
1/2 cup almond milk
1/4 cup olive oil or melted coconut oil
Zest of 2 lemons
1/4 cup fresh lemon juice
1 tsp vanilla extract
1 1/2 tsp baking powder
1/2 tsp baking soda
1/4 tsp salt

For the Lemon Glaze (Optional):
1/2 cup powdered sugar
1-2 tbsp fresh lemon juice

Allergens

CONTAINS GLUTEN   CONTAINS NUTS

INSTRUCTIONS

Preheat the Oven
- Preheat the oven to 350°F (175°C). Grease an 8-inch cake pan and line with parchment paper.

Mix the Wet Ingredients
- In a mixing bowl, combine the almond ricotta, sugar, almond milk, olive oil, lemon zest, lemon juice, and vanilla extract. Whisk until smooth and well blended.

Combine the Dry Ingredients
- In a separate bowl, whisk together the almond flour, all-purpose flour, baking powder, baking soda, and salt.

Combine Wet and Dry Ingredients
- Gradually add the dry ingredients to the wet ingredients, gently folding them together until just combined. Be careful not to overmix, as this can make the cake dense.

Bake the Cake
- Pour the batter into the prepared cake pan, smoothing the top with a spatula. Bake for 35-40 minutes, or until golden and a toothpick comes out clean.

Cool the Cake
- Cool the cake in the pan for 10 minutes then transfer to a wire rack.

Prepare the Lemon Glaze (Optional)
- Whisk powdered sugar and lemon juice for glaze

Glaze and Serve
- Once the cake has cooled, drizzle the lemon glaze over the top or dust with powdered sugar for a simpler finish.

CHEF'S TIPS

Extra Flavor: Add a dash of almond extract to the batter for a more intense almond flavor, or sprinkle slivered almonds on top of the cake before baking for added texture.

Variations: You can replace lemon zest and juice with orange for a different citrus twist or add blueberries to the batter for a pop of color and sweetness.

Vegan Zeppole with Powdered Sugar

Vegan zeppole are warm, fluffy Italian doughnuts, lightly dusted with powdered sugar and featuring a crispy exterior and airy interior. These plant-based treats offer a delightful texture contrast and a hint of vanilla sweetness, making them perfect for festive occasions or indulgent snacks.

Wine Pairing: Prosecco or a Sparkling Rosé

INSTRUCTIONS

Prepare the Yeast Mixture
- In a bowl mix warm almond milk, sugar, and yeast. Let sit 5-10 minutes until foamy.

Make the Dough
- In a large mixing bowl, combine flour, salt, yeast mixture, olive oil, and vanilla in a bowl. Stir into a sticky dough.

Knead the Dough
- Knead on a floured surface for 5 minutes until smooth and elastic.

Let the Dough Rise
- Place dough in a greased bowl, cover, and let rise for 1 hour until doubled.

Heat the Oil for Frying
- In a deep pot, heat about 2 inches of vegetable oil over medium heat until it reaches 350°F (175°C). To test the oil, drop a small piece of dough into the oil.

Form and Fry the Zeppole
- Scoop dough balls (1-2 tbsp), fry in batches for 2-3 minutes per side until golden.

Drain and Dust with Powdered Sugar
- Drain on paper towels, and while still warm, dust generously with powdered sugar.

Serve
- Enjoy warm with extra powdered sugar if desired.

CHEF'S TIPS

Extra Flavor: Add a pinch of cinnamon to the powdered sugar for a warm, spiced flavor or a hint of lemon zest to the dough for a citrusy twist.

Variations: For a more indulgent treat, serve the zeppole with a side of melted dark chocolate or a vegan caramel dipping sauce. You can also fill them with vegan pastry cream for a twist on the classic.

Difficulty

 15 min   20 min

INGREDIENTS

4 servings

- 1 1/4 cups all-purpose flour
- 1/2 cup warm almond milk (or other plant-based milk)
- 2 tbsp sugar
- 1/2 tsp salt
- 1 tsp vanilla extract
- 1 tsp active dry yeast
- 1 tbsp olive oil
- Powdered sugar, for dusting
- Vegetable oil, for frying

Allergens

CONTAINS GLUTEN

Varenna: The Romantic Gem of Lake Como

Nestled on the eastern shore of Lake Como, **Varenna** is a charming village that captures the hearts of all who visit. Known for its **romantic ambiance** and tranquil setting, Varenna offers a quieter, more intimate experience compared to some of the lake's larger towns. Its colorful houses, perched along the water's edge, create a postcard-perfect view that has made it one of Lake Como's most photographed destinations.

Stroll along the **Passeggiata degli Innamorati (Lovers' Walk)**, a scenic lakeside path that winds through the village, offering breathtaking views of the water and the surrounding mountains. Visit the **Villa Monastero**, a historic estate with stunning gardens that stretch along the lake, showcasing a blend of Mediterranean and alpine flora. Nearby, the **Castello di Vezio,** perched on a hill above the village, provides panoramic views and a glimpse into the region's medieval history.

Varenna's quiet charm, combined with its rich cultural heritage, makes it a must-see destination on Lake Como. For visitors, it embodies the romance of Italy, offering a peaceful escape where time seems to stand still. Whether savoring a glass of wine by the waterfront or exploring its cobblestone streets, Varenna is a place where memories are made.

Photo on the side: The village of Varenna, Lake Como

Acknowledgments

Creating Vegan Italiano: 50 Fresh Plant-Based Recipes from Lake Como – Authentic Italian Flavors Reimagined has been an incredible journey, and I am deeply grateful to the wonderful souls who have made this book possible.

First and foremost, I want to thank my wife, Marina. It was you who introduced me to the beauty and depth of the vegan lifestyle, and your unwavering support has been my anchor in every decision and every moment of my life, especially during the most challenging times. You have always stood by my side, and for that, I am endlessly grateful. Thank you also for your brilliant work on the graphic design of this book. You managed to create something far beyond what I could have imagined, bringing these recipes to life with impeccable artistry and style.

I also want to express my gratitude to the rest of our family—our beloved companions who have been with me every step of the way. To Kira, our affectionate little dog, who kept me company through long hours of writing and editing, always by my side with unconditional love. To Pika, our lively cockatiel, whose cheerful presence perched on the screen added a spark of joy to the process. And, of course, to Gordi, our melodic Fischer's lovebird, whose songs created the soundtrack to my work and filled the room with warmth and inspiration.

This book is part of the Fresh Plant-Based project, a labor of love dedicated to sharing the beauty of plant-based cuisine. If you're looking for more recipes, inspiration, and content, I warmly invite you to visit my website at freshplantbased.com.

This book is a celebration of food, love, and family, and I couldn't have done it without you all. Thank you from the bottom of my heart.

With love and gratitude,

Photo on the side: Villa Balbianello's Garden, Lake Como

General Index

Looking for more inspiration? Visit **freshplantbased.com** for additional recipes and ideas.

General Index

Craving more ideas? Head to **FreshPlantBased.com** for additional recipes and inspiration!

Alphabetical Index

Looking for more inspiration? Visit **freshplantbased.com** for additional recipes and ideas.

Alphabetical Index

Craving more ideas? Head to **FreshPlantBased.com** for additional recipes and inspiration!

Credits

Author:
Manuele Colombo

Photography:
All food photography and styling by Manuele Colombo.

Design and Layout:
All Design and Layouts created by Marina Fabre Morales.

Editing:
Edited by Manuele Colombo and Marina Fabre Morales

Recipe Testing:
Special thanks to Roberto, Marina, Davide e Beatrice for ensuring the recipes are perfect for every kitchen.

ISBN: 9798301487637

Publisher:
Self-Published by Manuele Colombo.

Website:
Visit **FreshPlantBased.com** for more recipes, updates, and behind-the-scenes inspiration.

Made in United States
Orlando, FL
12 March 2025

59407000R00081